M I R A C L E S   O F   T H E

B U R L I N G T O N
R E V I V A L

Bryson,
I pray that one day you will read this, you were there one night

MIRACLES OF THE

BURLINGTON
REVIVAL

CT TOWNSEND

Co-authored by Geoff Wasserman and Jordana Megonigal.

Photos by Heather Williams.

Published by The Brand Leader™
18 S Markley Street, Suite B
Greenville, SC 29601

First printing May 2018
ISBN 978-0-692-11433-9

CONTENTS

*Now unto him
that is able to do
exceeding abundantly
above all that we
ask or think,
according to
the power that
worketh in us.*

EPHESIANS 3:20
KJV

FOREWORD
Dr. Ralph H. Sexton, Jr.

When asked to share my thoughts about the Burlington Revival, I have to admit, I found myself at a loss for words.

How do we put into words the incredible works of our Lord?

How can we describe the things and people that were brought into the plan and purpose of God?

How do we put services into words that, at one moment demonstrated the glory of God, and a few moments later were saturated with conviction?

How can we adequately tell of a life changed by God, or a marriage put back together?

How do we begin to do that?

What I can say is that I believe the Burlington Revival is an example of what God can do when a church gets a burden to pray. It is how

God can reach the hearts of men, through the collective efforts of men and women who are willing to surrender and be used by God.

Revival is for the church, the redeemed, the followers of Christ, who want to see God move in the lives of their families and friends.

This type of meeting is used to encourage believers, remind the wandering of the way home, and for the lost to hear and see the light of The Gospel.

The importance of this meeting in Burlington was revealed in several ways.

First, the geographic location of the tent. It was at the roadside of I-40, one of the busiest roadways in the South, and people could drive from hundreds of miles just to attend.

Second, the impact on the spiritual temperature of our churches. We're living in a day when we could characterize that climate as lukewarm, at best. We have lost our tears and our burden for lost people!

Third, the social and cultural condition of our country. We have taken God out of our schools, removed public prayers to God, and have forbidden the Ten Commandments from being posted in our buildings!

As I write this in 2018, we are seeing our nation bear the fruit of a nation who has rejected the faith of our fathers, in the lives of our children and grandchildren.

That revelation never struck me any more than in my recent crusade in South Korea. Dr. Billy Kim and Far East Broadcasting opened the door for me to several of the world's largest churches.

I expressed to Dr. Kim and Dr. Paul Cho that I was so touched and moved with their people's burden to pray. Many of the services we had were at 5 and 6 a.m., yet, thousands would be in attendance! I asked them, and other pastors, how and why all these people would attend church every day, faithfully, before they go to work.

Dr. Kim's response caused an earthquake in my spiritual man:

> *"Dr. Sexton, here in South Korea, we're a lot like you were in America in the 1950s. We still love our parents and our grandparents. We care deeply about our families. The burden to care for each other and past generations, and for those to come is real love. We don't lock our front doors. We love one another and we honor God. We still have 5 a.m. and 6 a.m. prayer meetings. We also have a healthy fear of stopping, because we have seen what happened in your country, as America left the God of its fathers. That's why we're so fervent in our prayers for America and for us here in South Korea, because if America falls, there is no one to defend and protect us, so we desperately need God."*

You've heard people talk about passion in prayer. However, when a nation is praying for the physical protection of its families, that's a whole different story. When he shared this thought with me, it hit me like a ton of bricks: this was *America's* original story. America was built on that principle, and God has used churches, community revivals and camp meetings to keep our nation's feet on a faith foundation.

That's why, when you examine the history of our country and how God brought revival so many times to America, you realize the Burlington revival wasn't something new. That revival was just something new for this generation, for this time, for this season, because as a nation we've starved our children and grandchildren of our heritage.

As a nation, we were built on tabernacles. Those old wooden structures, with canvas stretched over them, mark a track record of God bringing revival to people, hearts into repentance, and people to a relationship with Him.

Even some of the pillars of our nation's educational system, like Yale and Harvard University, were founded with the intention of spreading the gospel. Harvard, which is considered our nation's most prestigious educational institution, and whose website today will tell you they ironically no longer have a formal mission statement, originally was founded in 1636 with the intention of establishing a school to train Christian ministers.

In accordance with that vision, Harvard's "Rules and Precepts," adopted in 1646, directed:

> "Let every student be plainly instructed, and earnestly pressed to consider well, the end of his life and studies is, to know God and Jesus Christ which is eternal life (John 17:3) and therefore to lay Christ in the bottom, as the only foundation of all sound knowledge and learning. And seeing the Lord only giveth wisdom, let everyone seriously set himself by prayer in secret to seek it of him (Prov. 2:3). Every one shall so exercise himself in reading the Scriptures

*twice a day, that he shall be ready to give such an account
of his proficiency therein, both in theoretical observations
of language and logic, and in practical and spiritual truths,
as his tutor shall require, according to his ability; seeing the
entrance of the word giveth light, it giveth understanding to
the simple (Psalm 119:130)."*

At every turn, you'll see our nation's foundations built upon
the principles of a Christ-centered life. From Shubal Stearns,
Alexander Marshall, and Charles Spurgeon, to R.G. Lee, Dwight
L. Moody, and so many more, revival has consistently marked
God's heart to bring His people back. In fact, Francis Asbury, the
great, tough-as-nails Methodist evangelist, traveled 250,000 miles
on horseback preaching over 25,000 sermons to spread the gospel.
That's our history as a nation—a heritage of revival!

Revival isn't just at the roots of our nation's history. It is our spiritual
DNA, and it's at the core of my family's history, as well. My father,
as a seventeen-year old boy, sat in back row of a tent meeting,
listening to the great evangelist William S. McBirnie. After service,
my dad was so convicted, he surrendered to the Lord right then
and there. He later turned down a basketball scholarship and went
on to graduate Bible college, and eventually became a missionary
to Africa for a short season. During WWII, Dad held God and
Country rallies under the "Gospel Tent". Later on in one of those
tent services, my Mom came one night and gave her life to the
Lord in my Dad's tent meeting.

Years later, when I was seven years old, my dad was leading a
packed-out tent meeting in North Carolina. With no seats left,
they asked all of the children to sit in the shavings. That night,

sitting in the shavings, the Lord spoke to my heart, and I trusted Jesus to save me. All three of us, spanning multiple decades, were saved in tent meetings.

Just as God used revival for my family all those years ago, I believe that same God was moving in The Burlington Revival as He has through so many revivals over the centuries. Today, that same "Hand of God" is alive and working to try to bring America's feet back to our faith foundation. We're seeing a mighty manifestation of God's hand touching people and places and hearts, to bring us revival in the midst of our bondage, and for His ultimate purpose and glory.

What, then, is the significance of the Burlington Revival? I believe it was so important at such a pivotal point in the history of spreading the gospel in America. We're in the midst of a global technology explosion, social media, online church, and so many things all happening in our world. Burlington reminded us of the simplicity of the Gospel. It challenged us to remember how we got here, and what God still wants to do *in* us, *around* us, *through* us and *in spite of* us. At Burlington, at its core, we saw the Hand of God, and the power of the Holy Spirit.

> *"Now faith is the substance of things hoped for,*
> *the evidence of things not seen."*
> — Hebrews 11:1, KJV

The beauty of what I saw in Burlington is what can't be seen. This scripture reassures me that because I have faith, that very faith is the evidence that guarantees me there's more to come that I have not yet seen. The bigger fruit is what will come forth out of God's word, the seeds sown and the obedience and sacrifices and prayers of that revival, over time. The harvest will not just be the salvations and the generational impact through the transformed lives of those who attended and made declarations for Christ. It will also be "the next CT Townsend" that God will bring forth from that ground, as a result of prayers and seeds and decisions sown in that fertile soil.

Now you know why years ago, as I sat in my office and a young man named CT Townsend said, "I believe I'm supposed to go into full time evangelism," I responded the way I did. That is what he believed God was calling him to do, after a time when he had faithfully served and been a blessing as one of my Associate Pastors at Trinity.

I was very burdened about CT going into full time evangelism. As you can imagine, I was concerned about losing him from our local church. If you're a pastor who loves your church and the people you serve and lead, you want God's best for them. Both CT and his wife Becky had poured out their gifts, both in our music and from our pulpit, and were an integral part of our church family. Understandably, in the natural, I knew it would appear to leave a hole in our week-to-week worship and service. But when I saw that fire and burden in him, and I remembered the gifts and callings of God are without repentance, it was less of a concern to lose him than it was to miss out on being a faithful part of what God was getting ready to do.

That's why my spirit leapt for joy for the next generation of people that were about to be forever changed. You see, over time as a pastor you realize that there's always another generation who needs someone else who's willing, and called, to go to the highways and the hedges, and tell the nation about Jesus. The answer isn't Republicans, Democrats, Independents, laws, or Congress...the only answer is Jesus, and that answer only comes by the preaching of God's word.

In the religious world today, we are seeing such an unhealthy competitive spirit about church size, how we do ministry, and all the trappings that come with that spirit. However, as leaders, releasing God's man and God's woman at the right time can be one of the most important things we can do, and I knew if we were both working toward the same goal, then it would bless our church for him to be successful.

I knew CT's heart, his burden, and his ultimate character and his desire to please God. So it was with that same spirit later, when Burlington broke out and Brother Hobbs needed a bigger venue and he called to ask about using our canvas cathedral, that we responded absolutely and unwaveringly by giving them our trailers and tent. Because of the history our church had with revival, I knew at that moment my job wasn't to want to preach at Burlington. It was to help CT go preach. If that meant that to see His power, His presence, and His person, I needed to lend him my tent and trailers, or carry his Bible, or bring him a glass of water, I was willing!

I learned that from watching my father, and so many other older preachers. Whenever they got behind a younger preacher who may have been just getting started, God blessed them as a result of their obedience. The Bible is pretty clear on God's instruction when it comes to being willing and obedient:

"If ye be willing and obedient, ye shall eat (inherit)
the good of the land."
— Isaiah 1:19, KJV

If the missions fields are the land, then it stands to reason that the spiritual harvest God wants us to reap is the people who are the harvest of that land, the fruit of the work of everything we do as a church.

"Lord, I'm willing" and "Lord, if it be thy will" both preach and pray well, until we're actually challenged to be obedient and put our willingness to the test. Those older preachers recognized that a part of *"the good of the land"* was the fruit that the next generation of preachers' work would produce. They saw it as their responsibility to sow spiritual seeds into that very land to produce a harvest of revival, and a next generation of preachers, who could lead a new generation to revival in a way that they themselves would not be able to lead in their lifetime.

I discovered that personally, years before, as a young Youth Pastor in the late 1970s. Back then, much like CT, I got a lot of invitations, and in 1980 I stepped out into evangelism. However, in 1988, my father suffered a massive heart attack. When it happened, I was in a crusade in Georgia, and my hometown church called me and asked if I'd come serve as Senior Pastor. I was happy and doing well, but I answered the call back to Asheville. When I arrived, I saw clearly that the local church was vital to sending evangelists out, and recognized the church's role in needing to solidify that calling and pipeline.

Today, our church is celebrating thirty years together. That could only happen because all those years ago in 1988, they accepted me and allowed me to make my green mistakes as a young pastor, giving me a wonderful gift very few leaders are afforded by their congregation: the freedom to fail. They also allowed me to grow the church into a place where we could raise up and release the next generation of preachers, pastors and evangelists—an assignment I believe is still on the church at large today.

So when it came to CT leaving our church, not only were the people not surprised, they were excited and expected it, because we had established a culture that expects to send people out. We see our role as a place to build them, bless them, train them, support them, and then we expect them to go into the world and preach the gospel into all the parts of the earth we can't reach on our own.

That's what the Burlington revival was about. After all, it started with the local church, and people at the local church praying all those years ago. New Hope Church didn't know if it would be CT Townsend or John Brown, but they believed revival was coming one day.

At a Pastors' conference a few weeks ago, the moderator asked me why in the world I'd loan my equipment, and my name, to a young evangelist. I asked him what he meant. He said, "You don't hear of that; why would you take the risk?"

My reply was simple: "Why *in* the world? Because my thinking wasn't *of* the world, so I didn't see it as a risk; it was an opportunity, and a blessing. I didn't respond to CT out of, *'what's best for my church.'* I responded out of what I believe God's vision is for His church…"

Imagine, if we all did that, what revival we might see in our lifetime.

ABOUT
DR. RALPH H. SEXTON, JR.

Since 1988, Dr. Ralph H. Sexton, Jr., has served as the Senior Pastor of Trinity Baptist Church in Asheville, North Carolina. Ordained in 1975, Dr. Sexton has an earned Doctor of Divinity from Bethany Theological Seminary in Dothan, Alabama, and honorary degrees from the Baptist International School of the Scriptures, Baptist Christian University, and Trinity Baptist College, Jacksonville, Florida.

He entered the field of full-time evangelism in 1980, holding crusades, seminars, and church revivals in America, Honduras, Haiti, Egypt, Israel, Jordan, Lebanon, Austria, Czechoslovakia, Germany, Mexico, and the Bahamas. At the invitation of the National Park Service, Dr. Sexton conducted a crusade on the National Mall in Washington, D.C. in 1986. Following in the footsteps of his father, he is a second-generation "righteous Gentile" in his love for the people and land of Israel, including forty-four trips to Israel and the Middle East, and serves on the Committee to Relocate the U.S. Embassy to Jerusalem.

*Pastor Randy Hobbs' burden for prayer helped
lay a strong foundation for revival.*

15 YEARS OF PRAYER
By Randy Hobbs

I've been the Pastor at New Hope Baptist Church for thirty-nine years, and we were honored for the Burlington Revival to begin at our church. I've been to some great meetings, but that was the greatest one we ever experienced at New Hope; we knew from the very beginning that it was a "God" thing, and we tried to be careful the entire time to give Him the glory and the honor. It may have been scheduled, but so much of what eventually happened could never have been planned.

I don't believe there will ever be revival unless people are praying. God works through the prayers of His people, and I felt like God had poured out a spirit of supplication on our church. He had laid it on my heart years before to just give one night—not our regular prayer night—but one night, every week, set aside specifically for us to focus on praying for revival. We had prayed for revival the entire thirty-nine years that I had been there, and we'd had some great meetings, but never had we dedicated one night every week for it.

So, about fifteen years prior to the meeting that would become the Burlington Revival of 2016, we began to pray. Every Monday night for fifteen years, that small group of people, a nucleus of people of our church, would be praying specifically for revival every Monday night, and claiming the promises of God.

James Stewart, a missionary from Britain who shook two continents, once said something that always stuck with me. He said, "God can send revival to any church, and to any group of people that will pray and claim the promises of God." God showed me that He honors faith, and I believe that He did. The part that we played? We were just consistent in praying.

As a leader, I had to consciously keep it on course, because as time went on people would want to pray for everything else. It took perseverance and unwavering commitment, because fifteen years is a long time for a church to keep up any program. We never had a large group of people praying, and sometimes it got just down to just a handful of us, continuing to pray for something that for all that time didn't come. But I do know this: the times we weren't praying, I could tell a difference in the atmosphere of our church.

As we were praying, I really didn't know what we were in for, and I really didn't expect that God was going to do to this—certainly not to the extent that He ultimately did, and is still doing as a result of the Burlington revival. We had had Brother CT Townsend visit for meetings before, and one time I had wanted to extend the time of the meeting, but he couldn't work it out because of prior commitments to other churches—other regions in need of revival—and understandably, we both wanted him to honor those commitments. So in 2016, I purposed in my heart: If God moves this time, we're going to extend it, whatever it takes. Fortunately, CT was in agreement with me to do that.

It was my privilege to moderate that meeting for those few weeks and I saw things up on that platform that I'll never get over until Jesus comes. I've never experienced the raw power of God like that—the drawing power of God—from the very outset. So we were just honored that God chose our church, that He honored our faith and the sacrifice that so many people made for so long to pray for this revival. We weren't by any means the only ones praying for it, but God honored us and I bless Him for it.

I like to think it's put our church at another level, and that our church will never be the same. I've got two preacher boys and a daughter and I'm glad to tell you they got to live to see something like that; to experience something tangible and real. Someone once said, "Once you've been in the fire, the smoke will never do." It's true; once you ever get that in you you'll never be able to get away from it.

Looking back, I can say—from experience now and without hesitation, not simply by faith—that *prayer goes to the heart of revival.* God works through preaching and God works through praying, and God showed me that He can do it again; that He's not out of business. That summer we saw something that we normally have only heard about and read about, but we actually experienced it. It reminded me that God is still God, and God still has all the power.

Teens gathered at Carolina Youth Camp in 2015,
almost a year before the Burlington Revival began.

THE FIRE FALLS

In studying revival, it is impossible to ignore the impact of young people being near the center of revival. There is something special, real and raw about a young person still too young to know how to "fake it," who gets his or her heart set towards the things of God. I have seen first-hand how God loves young people; He loves their worship, and He is attracted to their faith. Many have made the statement that they (the young people) are the church of tomorrow, but I'll argue that they're a major force in our churches today. The history of revival is permeated with the involvement, prayers and surrender of young people.

Throughout history, there were landmarks leading the way to what happened in Burlington, North Carolina, in 2016. In fact, it's interesting to note that this was not the first time Burlington experienced a move of God. Years ago, there was a great revival in Burlington under the ministry of Evangelist Mordecai Ham (1878-1959). Even in recent years, there were landmarks leading up to the Burlington Revival that most never saw. But every once and a while, one of God's miracle moments would reveal itself, and they now serve as beautifully woven markers on a timeline that we can look back to, reminding ourselves and witnessing to others about God's supernatural presence, power and purpose.

One of those moments happened about a year before the Burlington revival broke out, in a small mountainside camp known as Awanita, in Marietta, South Carolina. It was there that we had our Youth Camp that year, and welcomed around seven hundred and fifty youth to the area for a week of church camp, praise, prayer and preaching.

The week was great, but typical of the youth camps and events we'd experienced before. We had churches represented from all across the East Coast and beyond—from Illinois to Mississippi, Pennsylvania to Florida and so many more states in-between. But what was most memorable there happened the very last night of the week, and was a true showing of the power of the Holy Ghost to impact people of all ages and backgrounds.

All week long, I had been preaching on the life of Elijah—specifically from 1 Kings 18—and how the fire fell from heaven. I remember feeling so very burdened to convey the message of another generation rising up, to seek the face of God and to see the fire fall in their generation. We had no clue, however, of all that God had in store.

The last night, I walked into the chapel while a group was on the platform singing. I was over-prepared; I'd been studying all day, and I was ready to walk up to the front and start. But that day, as I would soon discover, God had other plans because He'd started without me. As I walked to the pulpit, it was as if the Holy Ghost nudged me. "Sit down." I didn't know why, and I surely didn't know what to expect, but I remember thinking: whatever is happening, I know it's God, and so I'll be obedient, not knowing what's on the other side of my obedience because that way, whatever He does, no one (including me) will be able to say that it happened because of me. So instead of continuing to the pulpit, I took a seat in the very back row.

While a group of young people were on the stage singing, "Sheltered," all of a sudden, the bottom fell out. Kids started rushing to the altars from everywhere, and from there it just turned into a pure Holy Ghost church. Kids praying; kids weeping; kids singing. There were kids that were known to be distant from God on the altar, crying. I remember one girl vividly: a Gothic girl with black hair, who was very troubled. She initially decided that she didn't want to be there, but sure enough, she ended up getting saved. Nobody was pumping it; nobody was priming it. It was real, and it was evident that God's Spirit was in that place!

Three hours passed. By that time we were quickly approaching midnight, and we were still in church watching these teenagers as the Holy Ghost descended upon that place. Several of the preachers had exhorted from scriptures, many made professions of faith, and some young men had surrendered to the call to preach; it was unreal. Despite the time, I remember looking at some of the pastors in attendance who had brought groups from their respective churches from across the country who I assumed, understandably, had to be thinking, "It's midnight and we still have to drive home tomorrow."

At first I didn't know what to do—how do you stop the Holy Ghost? And who would want to? But we had sung every song that we knew to sing; I had said everything I had needed to say. So I instructed them, "I'm not saying we're done yet, but go get with your own individual groups, and pray and ask God to let this Spirit go back to your churches and see the fire fall in your community."

At that moment as I released them to their pastors, in my heart I thought, "Whew, service is over; that was another great week at camp." But something else was happening. I saw different churches going in to different areas of that chapel praying, and soon after I began to hear a commotion outside. I thought I heard a loud roar at one point, but Heath Williams, our event director and a fellow evangelist, had gone out immediately to check to make sure everything was okay, so I let it be.

It wasn't too long before Heath came back. "You're gonna wanna see this," he said. I stepped outside, and revival had descended on that whole mountain. Although we had told them to get with their groups to pray, when they got outside, it went to a whole new level. I'll never forget walking outside under that moonlit sky, looking out and through the darkness seeing teenagers, unprovoked and unplanned, pouring their hearts out to God. Many were weeping—some shouting, some running. It was Holy; it was real and unlike anything I had ever been a part of in my life. Many of the leaders, if they weren't out there with their young people, stood speechless with tears streaming down their faces. Before we could even get our heads around what was going on, there were six hundred teenagers out in the middle of that field, with another hundred still inside the church. I remember noticing one specifically—a very dignified, well-mannered young lady, who had gotten word that one of her parents' battle with cancer was nearing an end. I watched her shout all over that field for nearly two hours, crying out to God. At my best, I cannot describe what all God did that night. I hesitate to even include this in the book, because you just had to be there. In the natural, we knew nobody had orchestrated or instigated it—it's hard enough to tell one teenager what to do and to follow, and even more difficult to get others to fall in line, much less seven hundred of them. There were no drums…no lights…no fog…no sound system…just hungry hearts and a big God! The sounds of singing and shouting were ringing through those mountains, and those kids took to that field like it was the Holiest place on earth. And you know what? Maybe it was that night. To them it was, because that night didn't end until two-thirty in the morning, with kids constantly hovering over the little rock altar we had built in the South Carolina mountains just that week.

Those of us involved that night trace Burlington's explosion back to that moment. Oh, and guess who the main group of young people were that led the meeting outside? Kids from New Hope Baptist Church, in Burlington, North Carolina. We believe there were some big prayers prayed that night, and looking back, God not only heard them, but He answered them. There are those who weren't there and would never believe it happened, but I'll tell you this: there was a supernatural breakthrough moment on that mountain, and it all started because those kids caught the fire, and when those teenagers went back to their churches, they took that fire with them. They rallied their churches and their peers, and prepared the way for God to shine on Burlington the next year.

I don't know why anyone would be surprised; every major revival that has ever been has started with young people.

"To look back upon the progress of the divine kingdom upon Earth is to review revival periods which have come like refreshing showers upon dry and thirsty ground, making the desert to blossom as the rose, and bringing new eras of spiritual life and activity just when the Church had fallen under the influence of the apathy of the times."

E . M .   B O U N D S

THE STIRRING
OF THE WATERS

What became known as the Burlington Revival didn't start out that way. We had no vision for a three-month long meeting, nor did we ever dream that over 1,250 people would walk an aisle and trust Christ. Of course it is the heart and prayer of nearly every evangelist that God would send revival, but we were just going into this like any other meeting that had happened—I would come in for about a week, preach every night and then leave to do the same thing somewhere else.

We started on Mother's Day of 2016. We had good crowds; there was a good spirit, and I had liberty to preach, but that first week wasn't "out of the banks," if you will. However, looking back there was a deeper work going on.

When I was a boy, I remember mother calling my brothers and me into the house for dinner. We had been playing outside, and we were filthy. She wouldn't even let us in the house with our dirty clothes on; she would make us go straight to the bathroom and wash up before we could come to the table. I believe God operates the same way, before we can experience revival.

Evan Roberts, the preacher God used during the great Welsh Revival in 1904, would make this claim in seeking revival:

1. Confess all sin
2. Remove anything questionable from your lives
3. Give yourselves completely in obedience to the Spirit
4. Publicly confess Christ

James backs that up with tremendous truth concerning revival:

"Draw nigh to God, and He will draw nigh to you. Cleanse your hands, ye sinners; and purify your hearts, ye double minded."
— James 4:8, KJV

There is no shortcut to revival. If we want revival, we must get clean. That is what happened the first week of the Burlington meeting—a week marked by people getting right with each other, and right with God. Getting right with God is one thing, but when people begin to turn to one another and ask for forgiveness, and true repentance breaks out, it has a way of clearing a pathway to unprecedented power in our prayer.

When we saw people getting right with each other and then getting right with God, we knew something very special was about to happen.

That Friday night of the first week stands out vividly in my memory. I don't remember what I preached, but I do remember the altars filling up. Some of the girls from Youth Camp the year prior had been praying and praying for their siblings to be saved. They were praying together, united in unwavering faith, and that week, it happened. So on Friday night, as we were getting ready to close out, one girl and her mother grabbed Brother Randy's wife, Mrs. Lisa, to go pray together to rejoice over the saving of their sister and daughter. When they started rejoicing, you could feel the shift. I looked at my wife and I said, "God is in this place!" Soon after, the altars filled up again with people weeping and crying out to God, burdened for their lost loved ones. Looking back, I find it quite significant that no one was praying for "revival"—they were simply praying for more of God.

That night, as they cried out for God, there was an immediate shift within a matter of minutes. As we closed out that Friday night, Brother Randy walked to the pulpit and said, "I know Brother Townsend has other plans for next week, but I just feel like God is not done with this meeting. You all help me pray, and we will keep you posted about next week."

When he got up and said that, I don't think it was because there was so much fruit that he knew we had to keep on. I believe it was an act of faith at that point—a slight nudge from the Holy Spirit—because it could have gone either way. I remember sitting on that decision, and tossing and turning over it. I had enough respect for Brother Randy's judgment to know that if he said we needed to go another week, he was following the leadership of the Holy Spirit. Also, I couldn't deny that I sensed something was going on. There was no doubt in my mind at that point that something was happening there.

At the moment Brother Randy said, "I don't think God's done," I'll be honest—my mind was made up to still go to Chattanooga; I had a prior commitment and had already set our travel plans.

Since then, many people have asked me how I knew to stay. I tell them that as I lay down in my bed that night, tossing and turning in the middle of the night, I came to the decision in my heart based on three things that convinced me to stay. First, God gave me an unexplainable peace in prayer. Second, I had a deep burden to see God do more. Third, I remember feeling that if I left Burlington at that point, I'd be sinning against God. I know that sounds extreme, but that is the only way I know how to explain it. From that point through the rest of the twelve weeks, that's how I knew, week-to-week, that we needed to keep on.

When something as powerful as that happens and you experience it enough to know when it's God talking to you and when it's not, it's easy to then quickly let thoughts and voices creep into your psyche and talk you out of it. Sometimes it comes from those opposed to you or the enemy. But a lot of times, it simply comes from the concern for letting other people down. After all, I was headed to Chattanooga because I felt months prior that God had opened a door there to go preach. So I called Pastor Bill Broom of New Haven Baptist Church, and let him know what was going on. I said, "I know you've promoted your events and promoted the fact that I'd be there, and I know you've planned and that took time and resources, and I know your meeting is important, but I need to humbly ask you to give me liberty. I feel like I'm supposed to stay right here in Burlington, and I don't know what that means for Chattanooga so I wanted to call you and talk it out." And Pastor Broom—he was an older gentlemen with the same heart for revival—he was kind to me in that moment as could be—not just in what he said, but how he said it. "Brother CT," he said, "If it was going on here I sure hope you would stay, too." So he forgave me of that commitment and we decided to keep the meeting going.

There was a lesson in that phone call I'll never forget. There are times in your life when you set your hands to godly plans and He blesses those things we set our hands to so we continue on. Sometimes, along the way, godly people who we love change their plans and on the surface it seems to impact us in a negative way. In that moment, it's easy to get caught up in our flesh and develop offense and resentment—even jealousy and pride—thinking what we're doing is more important than any reason someone might have for letting us down, if we're not careful. The gift that Pastor Broom in Chattanooga gave me wasn't just releasing me of the schedule conflict, but that he did it in such a sweet way that was regret-free, guilt-free, and I left the call believing he was as excited about what God was doing in Burlington as we were. That reminded me that just as he so quickly and wisely saw it wasn't about him, it helped me remember as I pressed forward in Burlington that it wasn't about me, either. It was about Kingdom business—about what God was doing.

Oh, how I remember the peace that flooded my soul! God was on the move, and it was the thrill of my life to be where He was.

After I got off the phone with Pastor Broom, I quickly went to Pastor Hobbs' office. He and his wife, Mrs. Lisa, were at the church early that Saturday morning preparing things for the Sunday morning service. I told Brother Hobbs that God had given me peace to stay, and that Pastor Broom had given me liberty. He instantly began praising the Lord, and we spread word that we would meet back on Monday night for week two.

The Bible talks in John 5 about the stirring of the waters, where the first ones who stepped into those troubled waters were healed. That night, we felt the stirring of the waters. We felt what happens when the burden to be healed—to be saved—becomes first and foremost in everyone's minds, when all God's people come together, aligned in prayer and believing for the same miracles. That burden for salvation has taken down governments, dethroned kings, and changed the very course of history. So we knew it could bring the power of God to Burlington and heal anything and anyone needing healing.

There's a principle there, for the churched and the saved to make themselves right with God. In fact, the Bible mentions that as a specific conduit for revival itself:

> *"If my people, which are called by my name, shall humble themselves, and pray, and seek my face, and turn from their wicked ways; then will I hear from heaven, and will forgive their sin, and will heal their land."*
> — 2 Chronicles 7:14, KJV

There's an old saying about the definition of insanity—doing the same thing over and over, but expecting different results. By applying this scripture to that principle, we can reason that if we keep doing exactly what we've been doing, we will keep having church as normal. But if we want to see God move supernaturally, we have got to be clean. If you want to see God to do the supernatural, there is a cost to pay. The doctrine of holiness is still in the Bible, so let's live our lives clean. If you've got problems with your brother in Christ, fix it. If you're mad with somebody at work, make that right. There's probably a million reasons in your head and maybe even your heart why it can't happen. But God said His mercies are new every morning, so why not today? Why not now; why not you, right where you are?

NEVER STOP PRAYING

One of the things we always talked about and we prayed for was that God would save key people through his work in Burlington. Whether you're in ministry or not, if your heart is for revival in your community or anywhere in the world, what we saw as a result of this principle can happen right where you are—whether you're on a missions trip in Africa, or planting a church in North Dakota, or anywhere in between. God is not a respecter of persons, and this approach to praying for revival can happen for you, so I hope it'll encourage you.

It wasn't that people who weren't people of influence weren't important. In fact, it's the very opposite. We desperately wanted to reach "whosoever will" but we were, as you are, limited in our reach, resources and relationships. Fortunately, the Holy Ghost has no boundaries. Throughout the Bible, you'll find a pattern of where God went after key people at very strategic times in both their life and the lives of the community they were in, because He knew the power of the ripple effect that would happen. There may be no greater example of that, in fact, than

Paul, who was notorious for crucifying Christians until one day, he met Jesus. When his life was transformed, the impact was a ripple effect that grew and continues to grow to this day. So part of our prayer time together was for God to touch key centers of influence through what He was doing through us in this revival; to create a ripple effect that would extend far beyond the length of time of the meeting, or the walls of the church, or the poles of the tent. We knew the Bible was clear on this, about how we overcome—not just by the word, but by the power of our testimony. So standing on that scripture and those principles, we prayed that He would specifically save people that, simply through their salvation story, would have a dynamic ripple effect on others around them in ways we could never reach people on our own.

In Burlington, one of those people was Clint.

Truth be told, Clint had the reputation of being one of the meanest men in Burlington. He was involved in all different kind of vices and destructive lifestyles. He was tough, he was mean and his heart was cold to the things of God. By his own testimony, he was one of the hardest men in Burlington. He was just a hard nut to crack, and honestly, there are probably some people out there who thought he was beyond God's reach. But the thing about Clint was this: Clint had a godly mother who believed in the power of prayer.

As lost as Clint was, his mama, Minnie Jones, was one of the most prayerful women in the church that we knew. And as hard as he was, he would still come to church sometimes, simply out of love and respect for his mother.

A year before the revival, Ms. Minnie died, and truth is, no one thought those church walls would ever see Clint again after her death. But on Mother's Day—which just so happened to be the first day of what would become the Burlington Revival—there was Clint, his second Sunday in a row, sitting in that church pew. "It's what my momma would have wanted," he said.

He was right. His momma wasn't waiting for him that day in the pews. But that day, God was.

This wasn't my first time preaching at New Hope, or to Clint. He was notorious for not moving during the invitation or for leaving early. The church came together that Sunday morning, excited about the meeting and for what God was doing. Clint had no clue what he had walked into that morning. There was something different in that church that wasn't there a week earlier. Jesus was in the house, and we were about to see our first major miracle of the Burlington meeting.

As the service went on that morning, we noticed Clint sitting there, weeping during preaching—crying and grabbing the back of the pews until his knuckles got white—but he wouldn't come forward. He just had such evil binding him; a resistance to God and His plan for his life. He refused to budge.

Finally at one point, I was up front preaching, and I heard a lot of noise coming from the congregation. I remember looking toward the left side of the church, and as I turned around I wondered if someone might have been having a heart attack or something, because there was that much commotion. As I turned around, I saw the unfathomable. There was Clint; he had exploded out of his seat. It was as if time stood still. Was he leaving? Was he mad? If Clint doesn't get saved this morning, in a service like this, what will it take to convince him?

To my amazement, Clint didn't try to leave that morning. He turned straight toward the altar. His face was as red as a tomato, tears streaming down his face, as if it was a sprint to the altar. He couldn't get there fast enough. This big, tough man had been melted by the power of the Holy Spirit! That whole church erupted when he came forward. I'll never forget it; he got up and nearly the entire church started following him like an army, escorting him down the aisle, as he moved toward the altar.

That moment, to me, was one of the early major breakthroughs in Burlington. We had prayed sincerely for key people to get saved, and we had prayed specifically for Clint to get saved.

When Clint got saved, that whole town heard the news.

Somebody once preached on the science of how sound never stops; it travels. That should make sense to believers who know that prayers aren't simply idle words; they're real, life-giving, tangible, life changing, supernaturally-charged pockets of God's miraculous power, and so things of substance don't just disappear, any more so than if you throw a ball up in the air, you wouldn't expect it to just evaporate. No matter how far the throw is, or how high or far away you feel like you threw it, it eventually has to land somewhere. And so it stands to reason that every prayer ever prayed has never stopped— it's just continued on through time and space and it's promised that it will never return void, so it lands filled with God's power to change and transform people, marriages, lives, situations, and even souls.

You see, there are some things you're praying for that will produce a harvest you may never see in your lifetime, but God's promise for that seed to produce will not fail, because God cannot lie. Through such a miraculous event like the Burlington Revival, beyond just the pulpit, you had potentially tens of thousands of prayers released about people, lives, communities, and the world around us. You can imagine the ripple effect we may not fully even understand, nor see the full manifestation of, for decades. One thing is certain: Ms. Minnie's prayers came true, even after her death.

For Clint, his mother's death didn't bring him to Christ directly. However, her memory, her prayers, her faithfulness for all those years definitely helped bring him there. There's another powerful principle in Minnie Jones' life story about faithfully praying for her son. She shared her burden with others and because of that, long after her death, a community of people cared for a son many of them didn't know, and many others of whom didn't know him very well, but they continued to pray for him and when his heart was ready, they made room for him and led him to the Lord.

Keep this in mind as you're praying for that person in your life who needs Christ, remember to also pray that God will surround that person with godly men and women who will look for opportunities to show them God's love.

"You never have to advertise a fire;

everyone comes running

when there's a fire."

LEONARD
RAVENHILL

IN ONE ACCORD

We had no clue what to expect as we entered into that second week. There wasn't ample time to promote it. There was no glossy revival flier at every cafe in town; all we had to rely on was word of mouth and our obedience to what God had told us to do. The first week, our largest crowd was approximately three hundred people. By Monday night of the second week, to our amazement, the crowd had doubled. There were at least 600 people in that auditorium, and it was electric. Word had spread that God was on the move, and people were coming from miles away to get in on it.

Leonard Ravenhill, a revivalist, once said, "You never have to advertise a fire; everyone comes running when there's a fire." That was one of the greatest miracles of Burlington; we never tried to market it, it just happened. No planning committees; no organizing days; no marketing strategy. God did it, and God got the glory for it.

That first week stands out in my mind because it was marked by the people of New Hope making things right with God and each other, seeking to get as clean as possible before God. The second week was so memorable for me because of how many local preachers and members of other churches came, and committed to getting things right with one another. Anyone who has been in or around ministry knows all too well the weapons that the enemy uses to keep the people of God divided. The very people that should be cheering each other on and fighting on the same team are often our greatest adversaries, and I personally believe that this grieves the Holy Ghost. But that second week, we saw pastors who would never before have even sat down and eaten lunch with another pastor, who were now so broken that they were on the same altar together, weeping for revival in their church and community.

When I was a child, nothing seemed to make my father more angry than when he would find us boys not getting along with each other. I believe the root of this is always our pride. Proverbs 13:10 says, "Only by pride cometh contention…" We can dress it up and give any excuse we want for hating or gossiping against our brothers and sisters, but it is sin in the eyes of God.

Please don't misunderstand me, not every pastor in or around Burlington got on board. Some held onto their grudges and opinions and negativity. I learned quickly that everyone wants revival, as long as it is at their church and they're the one preaching it. I believe God had to break this spirit of pride in Burlington before we could move forward.

I remember standing on the stage and watching men of God grab each other and dive into the altar together. As those men laid their hatchets down against each other, it was as if God had opened the windows of heaven. That second week was amazing, marked by God unifying the brethren in that area. The church was full, conviction was strong, and there was a powerful sense of a deeper cleansing going on in our hearts. We were in one mind and in one accord, working together, praying together and seeking the face of God together.

God was up to something much bigger than we saw or could imagine, and we were just thrilled to be a small part of it.

*Many gathered each night to worship and pray
as word of the meeting spread.*

WHEN THE BURDEN SHIFTS

Burlington started out the same way that most revivals do—with a lot of preaching about how big God is, and lots of sermons and songs about the love of God. It was the same thing that all of us had done for years, and everything was going well. But when people heard what had happened with Clint, there was a shift. People began saying things like, "Well, if God can save that guy, surely He can save my child." I even felt the burden change in my preaching from an exhorter that loved preaching a big God, to preaching what we call "revival preaching," pressing the notion and necessity of people "getting clean." It was very different, but it felt like a much stronger style of preaching that God directed us in, for that season, for that work He was doing. There was a different level of boldness in preaching, and I desired to be sensitive to it and conform to what God wanted. There are times that boldness can be misunderstood. It was not hateful or mean-spirited, but was effective in that time. There was so much God there, and so much liberty to preach, that the Word fell on good ground.

For me personally, over the past several years, God had geared my heart and ministry towards reaching young people. Whether in the Carolina Youth Rallies that we had started years prior, or youth camps and conferences, God had given us favor in that area and we loved ministering to and reaching young people. However, for a few years prior to Burlington, I had felt God leading me to steadily prepare and pray about a directional shift for the future of the ministry. In doing that, I remember God speaking to my heart in prayer one morning about how He was going to shift me from primarily having an audience with young people, to an audience with people much older and further along in life than me.

In the natural, that seemed like a daunting task. I remember thinking that I had no idea how God was going to do this; as a young preacher, I've always had an audience of young people. It was a natural (and supernatural) fit, and definitely a comfortable one. That's partly why it made sense to me that God would want that, He was preparing me to get way outside my comfort zone for much greater impact. I knew over the last couple of years that my assignment as I preached was, behind the scenes, to prepare my heart, my mind, my ministry, my family and my team for this shift because I believed God was going to open the door to it, and I knew when it came it would be too late to prepare. G. Campbell Morgan said something once that, to this day, always stirs my heart. "We cannot organize revival, but we can set our sails to catch the wind from Heaven when God chooses to blow upon His people once again."

I didn't know how or when God would let the wind blow, but I wanted to be as prepared as possible for the opportunity. Admittedly, I was intimidated by this shift, but many times in prayer and study, God would set my soul on fire in the book of Jeremiah and would overcome that any fear or intimidation I'd felt. My spirit bore witness with Jeremiah, because I had the same excuses. I'm too young; I'm not smart enough; they're not going to accept me, and on and on and on. But I remembered the conversation between God and Jeremiah:

> *"Then said I, 'Ah, Lord God! Behold, I cannot speak: for I am a child.'" But the Lord said unto me, 'Say not, I am a child: for thou shalt go to all that I shall send thee, and whatsoever I command thee thou shalt speak. Be not afraid of their faces: for I am with thee to deliver thee' saith the Lord. Then the Lord put forth his hand, and touched my mouth. And the Lord said unto me, 'Behold, I have put my words in thy mouth. See, I have this day set thee over the nations and over the kingdoms, to root out, and to pull down, and to destroy, and to throw down, to build, and to plant.'"*
> — Jeremiah 1:6–10, KJV

At Burlington, seemingly overnight, that opportunity became reality. I recall feeling amazed, shocked and humbled that these seasoned preachers and faithful saints of God would take the time to come hear such a young man as myself preach. I remember feeling unqualified, and not fit for the task. I even called Pastor Sexton one night weeping and telling him, "We need to get a real preacher in here now; I can't do this, this is over my head." But somehow, it seemed as if my whole life had led to this moment, and I praise the Lord for allowing me to be a part of the Burlington meeting.

*"Oh! Men and brethren,
what would this heart feel if
I could but believe that there
were some among you who
would go home and pray for a
revival. Men whose faith is large
enough, and their love fiery
enough to lead them from this
moment to exercise unceasing
intercessions that God would
appear among us, and do
wondrous things here, as in the
times of former generations."*

CHARLES
SPURGEON

THE PRAYERS THAT FUEL REVIVAL

In studying revival and great moves of God, I was always fascinated by the stories of great prayer warriors who stood behind and prayed for men of God while they preached. I remember hearing and reading stories of the Great Awakening and how people would pray and see God move in a powerful way. My mentor, Dr. Ralph Sexton, Jr., had told me stories of men who had prayed for him through the years, and how intercessory prayer was always the fuel for the fire of revival. E.M. Bounds said, "Talking to men for God is a great thing, but talking to God for men is greater still."

One night, a seasoned pastor walked up to me, and we began talking about intercessory prayer. He made this statement: "If this meeting is going to go to the next level, we're going to need dedicated intercessory prayer." I had never had that. I have had people pray for me, but never on the levels he was speaking of that day.

That's when the phone call came from my friend, Evangelist Heath Williams. Heath was heavily involved in the meeting, and had a great burden for prayer, and that day Heath shared with me that he had received a phone call from one of his mentors, Pastor Daniel Buchanan. I knew of Brother Daniel, and he knew of me, but that was as deep as our relationship went at that point. I knew he was a good, solid, Bible-believing man, with a reputation of a man that knew how to pray. Heath told me that Brother Daniel had called him asking strange questions. Apparently, he had been off praying for days in Myrtle, Mississippi, and had told Heath that while he was in prayer, God laid Burlington on his heart. Not knowing anything about what was going on, but knowing Heath lived close by, Daniel asked Heath if he had heard of anything. Heath immediately told him what was happening, and said he began to hear Brother Daniel weeping and praising God.

I'll never forget the night Brother Daniel walked into that Burlington meeting, because he is a big, strong man from the mountains of North Carolina. He's one of those guys that, when he walks into a room, his presence—both spiritually and physically— can be very intimidating. However, he's as humble and kind a man as any you'll ever meet. He's a giant in stature like Goliath, but also in faith like Daniel. I remember it as clear as day: He walked in, sat on that front row, and the whole time I was preaching, he had his head back praying.

All of a sudden, I noticed he'd started smiling, and people began walking down the aisle to get saved. There's no doubt that God brought him on board; it wasn't like we said, "Hey come on, let's sign a contract to bring you into this." But Daniel got there at every day around four o'clock, and he'd get to praying under the stage in that sawdust, in the high temperatures of that summer heat. I recall feeling so overwhelmed that he would come at all, let alone pray for me.

I'll never forget that night in the service as God began to move and Brother Daniel smiled as if he was recognizing that God was there. From that night on, Brother Daniel stayed in Burlington with us and prayed...and prayed...and prayed. There's no telling how much hell he prayed off of us, and how much Heaven he prayed down on us. I am forever grateful that God sent him our way. If prayer is the key (and I believe it is), then Brother Daniel being in Burlington was just as much a miracle as anything else, and to this day we believe it to be the link that God supernaturally put in place.

"When Holy God draws near in true revival, people come under terrible conviction of sin. The outstanding feature of spiritual awakening has been the profound consciousness of the Presence and holiness of God."

HENRY BLACKABY

THE DRAWING POWER OF GOD

As we began the third week, word had spread throughout the community and surrounding areas. Multiple thousands of people were viewing the services online. The talk of the town was the revival down at New Hope, and what God was doing. People would arrive at the church by 4:30 in the afternoon, and some nights it would be filled to capacity within an hour. People were being seated anywhere the ushers could put a body. The auditorium was filled, as were Sunday school rooms, foyers and back side rooms without so much as a view of the pulpit. Yet people came, night after night.

By this point there was such a liberty to preach on salvation, people were actively inviting friends, family and co-workers and were under a great burden to see them saved. It seemed as if every night I would run straight to Calvary, and people would walk the aisle. We would take a Bible and show them how to be saved, and many trusted Christ. There was so much victory in that room. God was on the move.

In many churches today, salvation has become one of the last things we preach, instead of the first. There are some that have even called it shallow, but shouldn't the greatest push of our day be to clearly present to Gospel? Eternity is too long to be wrong.

I'm thankful for my days in Bible College under Dr. R. Larry Brown at the Victory Baptist Church in North Augusta, South Carolina. Before we ever got a chance to preach in a church behind a pulpit, we had to be faithful preaching in places like the prisons and rescue missions. It was in those prisons in my early twenties that God taught me how to preach to sinners. Not arrogant or rude; not screaming at them and telling them they're going to hell; but with compassion, a genuine tear in our eye, warning them of the judgment that is to come, and a savior named Jesus, who paid the penalty of sin for them, and about a salvation that is available to "whosoever shall call."

In Revelation 20 we read about the Great White Throne Judgment, where all who have rejected Christ will appear for their final judgment before they are thrown into the lake of fire. The Bible speaks of this great summoning that will happen as mankind is brought to this judgment.

> *"And I saw the dead, small and great, stand before God."*
> — Revelation 20:12, KJV

Have you ever wondered who all will be judged at this Great White Throne Judgment? We should be prepared to preach to them all, and warn them of this coming judgment. However, I believe knowing who they are will help us as we attempt to reach them with the Gospel, so I'll break them up into four distinct crowds. During Burlington, I did my best to try to cover all four of these as I preached to sinners.

1.   **The Sinner and the Scoffer Crowd**

This is the crowd that we all know will be there. Those who hate God. Those who hate Christ. Those who hate Christians. In this crowd I see the worst of the worst. The deepest of atheism, those who burned Christians at the stake, the vilest murderer. As I look through the text I see this crowd standing there. But remember, there will not be one single atheist left at this time. They will all be firm believers in God at this point.

2.   **The Self-Righteous Crowd**

This crowd is absolutely shocked that they are even at the Great White Throne Judgment. They really believed that as long as their good works exceeded their bad works, everything would turn out fine in the end. America is full of these good ol' boys and good ol' girls who are trusting in their own self-righteousness to get them to heaven. But may I remind those belonging to this crowd that if your good works could have gotten you to heaven, than Jesus would not have had to die upon the cross.

3.   **The Someday Crowd**

As I see this crowd through the text, I see a look of panic, as they finally realize they have waited too long. These are the people that have heard the Gospel and had the best of intentions of *someday* getting saved. It is a frightening thing to think of how many people are in hell right now, at this very moment while you read this book. People in hell that had the best of intentions, after they sowed their wild oats, of a day when they would make things right with God. The danger is, for many, that day never comes.

4. The Sunday Crowd

This is the crowd that may have religion, but have no relationship with Christ. A form of Godliness, denying the power thereof. Jesus spoke specifically about this crowd in Matthew 7:21–23:

> *"Not every one that saith unto me, Lord, Lord, shall enter into the kingdom of heaven; but he that doeth the will of my Father which is in heaven. Many will say to me in that day, Lord, Lord, have we not prophesied in thy name? And in thy name have cast out devils? And in thy name done many wonderful works? And then will I profess unto them, I never knew you: depart from me, ye that work iniquity."*

God help us to preach with such power and truth to awake those who have been rocked to sleep by religion.

Preaching salvation to the lost is one thing. It's simple and straightforward. But preaching salvation to lost churched people is a whole other story.

I know, on the surface, for the unchurched, that might sound odd: 'lost churched people'. However, if you've spent a few years in church, and especially if you've been part of leadership in ministry, you know good and well if we were to go to any town in the United States this week where a church culture exists, and ask, "Are you a Christian?" most people who grew up in that town will probably say yes. Ask them how they know, and you'll get answers like, "My grandpa's a preacher down the road," or "I was baptized when I was a kid," or "For as long as I can remember, my family's been members of..." We're full of religion and traditions of attending church, but so many times, sadly, empty of Christ.

Unfortunately, our churches are set up to be comfortable places where the lost can be churched, people can be active members, and from the outside looking in and from all appearances, life is good, the church is alive and well and nobody's the wiser. However, let a storm hit, and suddenly you'll find that things aren't necessarily all they're portrayed to be. In fact, the late Southern Baptist evangelist, J. Harold Smith once estimated that seventy percent of a given church's formal membership was unsaved. Seventy percent. It's what happens over time, much like erosion. Ever go hiking or walking through the mountains and come across a rock that has been worn and damaged by the effects of erosion? Thousands of years ago, that same rock was full in shape, unweathered. What happened with erosion? Slowly, over hundreds of years, every drip of water, every storm, battering of hail, beating down of the hot sun, and other weather elements erode the rock over time. If it were possible to hold it up today next to a picture of how it looked in its intended, original, created state, you'd wonder how in the world it got to the condition it was now in. That's how religion can erode a life, a church, a community, and a nation. So many times in churches across America today, sadly, church has become a place where we preach for five hours, and pray for five minutes, and wonder where God is.

In the Burlington revival, as the burden shifted more to leading the lost to Christ, we shed a lot of the restricting, limiting factors and circumstances that modern-day churches feel, understandably, they have to consider. The problem comes when over time, it moves from consideration to being governed and confined by those same factors. You know the drill: you can't have church late on weekdays because there's school in the morning. You can't preach for too long or people will get bored. You have to be done at eight or you'll lose people. The restaurants close for lunch by two o'clock and the food on the buffet gets that glazed-over look and they'll blame it on you, pastor, for going too long. So we begin to erode the very wineskin we then want God to fill with new wine, and we wonder why the same people continue to hurt, the same problems never get resolved, and we become disheartened by how rarely we have a move of God in church. That was another powerful lesson learned in Burlington because we decided not to allow those factors to limit us; it was a decision. All of those limiting factors fell away and we replaced them with a commitment to focus on the things we believed that God wanted from us.

On meeting nights at Burlington, everything was quick until you got to the formal invitation for people to give their lives to Christ, and at that point, nobody rushed. We didn't leave until the lights turned out and every person who wanted to respond to the Gospel had their opportunity. Of course there are those who would say, "They just kept that invitation running all night," to which my response was always the same: "Would you like me to kick the people off the altars?" We never held the invitations open with no one at the altar, but as long as people were getting saved, we would have stayed all night! Sometimes that meant we didn't leave that tent until midnight or later. Sometimes that meant families were getting home at eleven at night, hadn't eaten dinner and hadn't done schoolwork. But no one minded. And in fact, the revival grew, week after week. And the most amazing part was that we didn't have to manufacture that, or try to make it happen, because God did it. He only asked us for one thing, really: obedience. As we discovered, there's amazing truth in His promise in Isaiah:

"If ye be willing and obedient, ye shall eat the good of the land."
— Isaiah 1:19, KJV

There was a hunger in all of us, our leadership, and those who came from all over the country, and many who watched around the world online. And through that willingness and obedience, we saw many eat the good of this land, this of salvation and revival, that God had prepared. Being and staying sensitive to what God is doing and what He wants next isn't always easy, but I've always found that it's incredibly rewarding. God is the same God that He was 100 years ago, but I fully believe that God has tried to initiate a lot of things in a lot of places, and many times we just miss it because we're so set on the boundaries we've put in place for ourselves, our churches, and our worship.

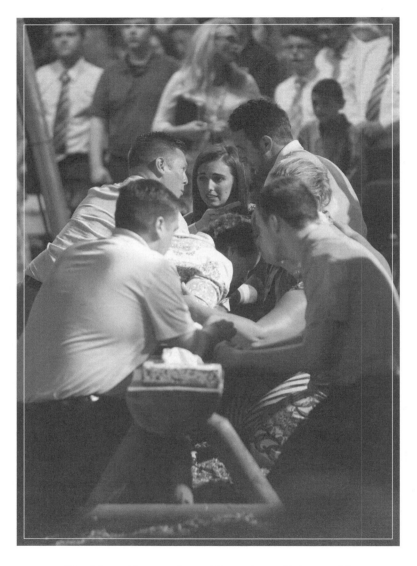

"And he said unto them, 'Go ye into all the world,
and preach the gospel to every creature.'"
MARK 16:15, KJV

REACHING
A NEW
GENERATION

One of the most unique things we saw with Burlington that we had never experienced to that measure in meetings before was the reception of the message from people across the globe who saw what God was doing there, due to the fact that we used social media to share what was happening. In doing so, people could connect with us, right where they were, and experience revival together. Never before had there been a tent revival that used social media or tools like live, streaming video to share all the details, in real-time, of what God was doing there.

If you look at a major media company, they may often have something like twelve to fifteen hundred people watching their updates live at any given time. But at Burlington, our livestream was constantly hitting thousands of people and more; by midnight, it was commonplace for each video to have over a hundred thousand views by the next day.

In the book of Mark 16:15 we read: "Go ye into all the world, and preach the gospel to every creature." To be honest, "*into all the world*" sounds like a pretty tall order, but it is possible, or the Lord would not have asked it of us. The question then becomes, for many of us, "I am one man, how can I reach the world?" I know that the internet and social media have their downsides and traps, but hear me out: in the 21st century, it is currently the most effective tool we have to get our message into all the world faster than ever before.

In Burlington, we used Facebook and other social media for all kinds of moments. We streamed each sermon and each service. We captured the moment that people cried out to God for salvation. We spent a bit of time each day updating our followers—who were located across the globe—simply to connect with them and share perspective on how God was moving, and how we were responding.

A preacher once told me this: "The fame of revival spreads the flames of revival." With every story and testimony of lives changed, each one built the faith of God's people to believe that God can still move in this day! Each update, within seconds, was broadcast across the world. It wasn't the ideal substitute for the real thing, but it served to connect the miracles happening in North Carolina with people from Tennessee to New Zealand, and everywhere in between, and to be a catalyst for revival breaking out in homes and churches across the globe—many of which we may never hear about in our lifetime.

BEATING THE STRONG MAN

On the last night of the third week of the revival, we walked into the church, and the place was packed. Chairs were put out all the way to the bottom step of the altar. I was nervous, because if I'm being transparent, I just didn't have peace in my heart at that point about what I was supposed to preach.

It wasn't that I hadn't adequately prepared to preach, it was just that I wasn't settled on what God wanted me to preach that night. I remember my hands shaking as I stood before this massive crowd, with seemingly nothing to say. But in that moment, that still small voice whispered, "The Strong Man."

The Strong Man? What do you mean the Strong Man? I looked over at Heath, who was sitting on stage, and I whispered to him, "Find me that verse in the Bible about the strong man!" I asked a man to pray while Heath faithfully scrambled trying to find the verse.

And then, he found it. I'd never studied that passage beyond surface level reading, and I had sure never preached from it, but off I went, and as I preached it God gave me the whole picture of what I was destined to preach that night:

> *"No man can enter into a strong man's house, and spoil his goods, except he will first bind the strong man; and then he will spoil his house."*
> — Mark 3:27, KJV

The basis was this: The devil has a stronghold on our nation, on our churches, and on our families today, and if we're going to experience true revival, we have to break the power of the strong man. To illustrate it, I took my son, Tucker, who at that point was all of about five years old, and I wrapped him in the arms of Pastor Hobbs, who was the biggest man on the stage. As he held Tucker tight, I said, "Don't you let him go, now. You're the Strong Man; a picture of Satan."

I stood up in front of the church and spread my arms wide. "I'm the father of this kid. Maybe he's addicted to drugs, maybe sin has a hold on him; he's in trouble, but the bottom line is he's in a mess and is bound by the power of the strong man." Then, I took Tucker's arms—still wrapped in the arms of the strong man—and started to pull on them. "Quit living that way." I pulled on Tucker's other arm. "Follow these twelve steps to get free, Tucker." I was illustrating how powerful the grip of the enemy is, and how powerless our man-made remedies are to free our loved ones from the strong man's grip. I pulled on him, I tugged on him, I hugged him, I wept over him. I did everything in my power. Nothing was working; my child was still bound tightly in the grip of the strong man.

I turned to the congregation, with tears streaming down my face, with the desire of a father to see his son free from sin. "Here's the thing," I said, "I cannot beat the strong man on my own. He is stronger than me. He is more powerful than me. He is smarter than me, and I am not a worthy opponent for him by myself. I cannot physically loose my son from his grip. So, when I can't beat the strong man, I've got to find a stronger man."

In the first few rows there was an even more massive man there. I went and got in front of him as if he was Jesus (The Stronger Man). "Jesus, my baby's in a mess. My kid's in a mess. I can't get him free; His momma and I have tried everything! I beseech Thee, I beg Thee, please, I need You to set him free." At that moment, that man, although unplanned, knew what I was doing, and ran on that stage with me, and broke the strong man's grip off of Tucker, and picked Tucker up.

In that moment, that place came unglued. I never got to preach any further because that scripture and illustration rang true in that place that night, and people started coming to the front to be saved. I remember it as one of the most powerful nights of the meeting as God did a real work in Burlington that night.

Everybody's got a family member that's addicted to something. Everybody knows what that struggle is like. But if we're going to live in victory, we have to get that stronghold broken.

After that night, everything changed. I'm pretty sure that without that night, there might not have been much more revival. I would've preached a message, had some impact, and we would've missed God's will. That night, the revival went from being a great meeting with pockets of people getting saved each night, to completely changing the entire scope of what we saw. It was what we called a breakthrough night.

There was such power in that room that night, that I know it could only have been from the Holy Spirit. A young lady in the room that night had been dealing with some severe demonic stuff—she had lost her marriage, and nobody could reach her—but that night, she ran to the altar, with tears running down her face.

That's what we found that night. People praying like never before. From that night forward, people continued to pour in, expecting to hear the chains fall off. Those precious people were so engaged, burdened for more of God, they were literally praying around the clock in shifts. They were praying some big prayers, and God was about to send some big answers.

THE UNITY OF LEADERSHIP

"Behold, how good and how pleasant it is for brethren
to dwell together in unity!"
— Psalm 133:1, KJV

The challenge with the rapid growth of Burlington was that as attendance expanded, the church walls did not. New Hope could comfortably hold around six hundred people, and we were packing around a thousand people each night in that building. Pastor Hobbs and his men were afraid that we were going to get in trouble with the fire marshal due to the crowds. We had people packed everywhere, stacked in every corner and even in every closet at that church by that point—far beyond the permitted number to be there at one time.

It appeared we'd run into another wall. What could we do now? We knew that we were going to have to do something else so we called different facilities in Burlington and Greensboro, but all were booked solid, since it was graduation season across the region. Pastor Hobbs thought about calling Dr. Ralph Sexton, Jr., of Trinity Baptist Church in Asheville, North Carolina, a well-known evangelist who had his own tent and equipment, and so we decided to give him a call. But even as we were following that path, I was concerned. I was worried about the heat—here we were in the South going into the hot summer months, where days can reach ninety degrees in the morning easily, and push into the high nineties and even hundreds by midday. But more than that, I was worried about the money. If you've never had to rent a large tent for a major event or revival, you wouldn't think there was much cost other than, of course, the large expense of a tent. However, with a tent of the magnitude we needed, tents are a money pit. There is so much to do—from finding land to lease, to running electrical, to grading for parking, renting chairs, insurance, and more.

We had a big problem and I knew we couldn't do it alone. Fortunately, we had a bigger God.

One night, after the meeting, we made an announcement that we were going to have a meeting specifically for the local pastors, over at the local Golden Corral, to discuss the direction and future of the meeting. Now, getting two pastors to sit down together can sometimes be a challenge because there's so much territorialism between most ministers. But that day, fifty-two pastors showed up for that meeting. Fifty-two. We were absolutely amazed at the unity of those pastors. At that point, while my name was all over that revival's promotions and meetings, I hadn't really preached around that area a whole lot. In Burlington and surrounding regions however, Randy Hobbs is one of the most respected pastors, and has been for a very long time. Over the years, he had faithfully earned the respect and love of those around him. Thankfully, those who weren't sure about this young evangelist had an established track record of trust with the seasoned Pastor's judgment, and trusted him once again.

So in that small town, in a Golden Corral, in front of fifty-two pastors from many different churches and cities, Brother Randy got up in front of that group of pastors and said, "God's done this, but it's grown to the place where this can no longer be just a New Hope meeting. If it's going to go to this next level that we really believe God wants, it has to transcend New Hope and become the burden of the surrounding churches as well. It's got to be the burden of all of us."

As Brother Hobbs spoke, I surveyed the room, looking at the faces of the preachers. Different men, from different churches, and not everyone there agreed on everything. However, that day, there was such unity concerning what God was doing in that town in that moment, they unanimously wanted to be involved. He put the mantle of ownership on those pastors to share that burden, not only emotionally and spiritually, but financially, too. And that was something that only God could do.

In retrospect, there were probably very few people through whom He could do it other than someone like Randy Hobbs at that moment, in that season; he had earned that credibility in the thirty-five years he had worked and prayed and preached in that community. Pastor Tyler Gaulden, of Church Street Baptist in Greensboro, later said, "The truth was, I could not have stood up at the Golden Corral and said that. Those pastors probably wouldn't have even come if it was anybody else other than Brother Randy."

That day was humbling because of how sovereign it was—for all of those years when he didn't think anything was going on, God was placing Brother Randy at the forefront of that community, for this one meeting, just so he could stand up and say, "This is no longer New Hope's meeting; God's in this for the community," and everybody would say, "Yeah, we agree." It was almost like Brother Randy took the keys to the very thing he'd been praying about for fifteen years, and said, "I've prayed for this; I've labored for this; but if you wanna get involved, I'm gonna give you the keys."

That's a principle that I believe God established long ago, when He declared that Jesus was His Son, with Whom He was well pleased. There wasn't a specific reason why He had to do that publicly. After all, He was God; He could've willed anything to happen that He wanted. But I believe He was showing us the power we as believers have of public affirmation of another. There's something that happens when an honored leader publicly affirms another with His mantle of leadership and honor, paving the way for His will to be done through the quick acceptance of that newly affirmed and appointed leader. In fact, it's probably one of the reasons why companies and churches don't transition well to the next generation; the outgoing leader doesn't recognize the power in honoring the one set to take the mantle of the next season of the move of God in that place.

Because of Randy's influence that day, something amazing happened. Every single one of those pastors stood up and pledged themselves and their churches in support of the Burlington revival. It was truly a God moment and a miracle to have that many pastors come together under a common purpose—they were unified. I also recognized something else that had come to fruition in that moment. Years before, I had worried when God told me my ministry would shift, and that I would move to just reaching youth to reaching many others, including leaders, much older than me, not just out of false humility, but truly out of a limited understanding of how God could use what limited ability and gifts I thought I had. If you had told me that was one of the pivotal ways He'd do it, I would've told you that you were crazy; that it could never happen.

And yet in that room, those pastors moved from hearing to agreeing, to weeping; they then moved from weeping to affirming and shouting; they even began praising and singing. The old hymn, "Brethren We Have Met to Worship" got started by one of the older pastors, and it sounded amazing coming from that group. If you had been in that Golden Corral that day, I promise you'd have been disappointed every time you ever visited a Golden Corral again, thinking it was just part of their dining experience in the South. Those people in that front room were looking back there trying to figure out what was happening, but we didn't care. Whatever was going on in that meeting had us all sitting there weeping and praising God that we were privileged enough to see what we've only heard other people pray about. That restaurant, we would later discover, would be just one exit down the highway from the site on which thousands would forever have their lives changed through their encounter with Jesus Christ.

The pastors came to that meeting because they wanted more from God for their churches, their city, their world and for the entire Kingdom of God, and a rare alliance was formed that night. We needed to raise about twenty thousand dollars that day to get the tent and all its parts moving, and within five minutes of Randy's speech it was all on the table. Every dime was raised, and we didn't have to beg for it.

That day showed me the true meaning of unity, and the limitless resources and ability God has to see His purpose and His vision come to life. I used to think that unity was if you and I sat down to talk; maybe we disagree on some things, but we can at best agree to disagree and move toward a common cause. But real unity doesn't even mean that you and I have to have a conversation together; it's God working in your heart and God working in my heart, to where that common line just happens.

A lot of meetings get to a certain point, and then the preachers shut them down because the preachers get in the way. Somebody thinks, "Well, Brother Randy gets to do all the talking at night", or "Well, my church hasn't been asked to do something" and then there's discord. But at Burlington, every man said, "I don't care if I just sweep the stage at the end—I'm just glad that God is here."

And that's why it didn't stop.

Every single week—if not every day, and at times it felt as if it was hour-to-hour—there was a test that the devil sent that could have easily destroyed the unity, grieve the Holy Spirit and maybe even ruin what was happening. There were situations that arose that, had we had operated in our flesh, could have destroyed the unity. God gave us insight to understand where the opposition was really coming from. The enemy was not another brother; the enemy was Satan, trying to find a way in. The men in leadership made a pact from the beginning to do our best to handle things correctly, with a right spirit, to preserve unity and ultimately not grieve the Holy Spirit. Through it all, every one of us knew that we may never see anything quite like this again in our lifetimes, so we had to love on purpose, for a greater cause and for a greater united vision than ever before.

And because of that conscious effort of the leaders to love and to seek God in every little thing, there was never a hint of division between any of us. We prayed together. We worked together. It was a joy. This was not a meeting of seeking our own glory, or creating a name for ourselves. Instead, it was literally, "God is doing this thing and we are just glad to be here."

In times like these, there has to be a higher purpose, or you lose track of the true meaning that it all has for God's kingdom. It has to be bigger than a paycheck; it has to be bigger than you. For us, this was what we had prayed for. It was an opportunity that was so big that it was not only going to touch us in the moment, but was going to transition our lifetime and the lives ahead of us. Every night, we came with huge expectations, yet God still did something every night that amazed us. Whether it was somebody's soul that He saved, or two preachers that didn't get along together being seen on the altar praying together, it was a supernatural unity that no one could deny.

I grew up all my life in the Independent Baptist movement, and at times, I felt like we weren't even allowed to like or fellowship with anyone outside those lines. But Burlington was different. Although the leadership consisted of Independent men, the crowd was not. I remember seeing Southern Baptist, Independent Baptist, Presbyterians, Church of God, Methodist, non-denominational churches, and many more. For the first time in my life, it wasn't about *my* church or *their* church; it was about what God was doing in that city, for those people. I believe that's one reason people would walk in and say, "This is real. This is God." Only God can unify people, crucify our pride, keep down strife and contention, and unify His people towards a common goal.

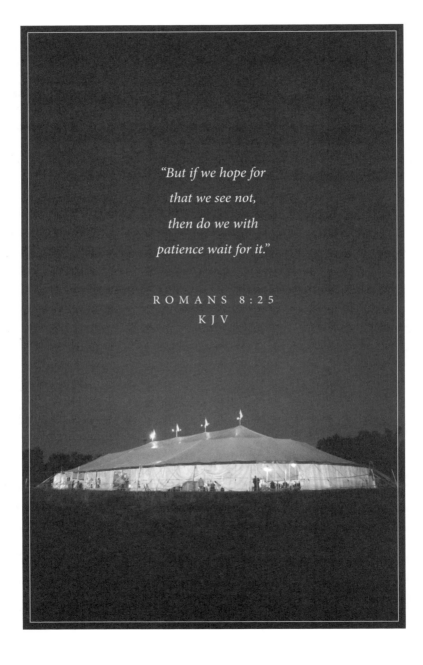

"But if we hope for
that we see not,
then do we with
patience wait for it."

ROMANS 8:25
KJV

THE MASTER ARCHITECT

Whenever God does big things, it's a whole lot easier to see the big picture after all is said and done, when you can reflect on how everything came together in a supernatural way. Sometimes, if you're truly blessed, you'll get to see the pieces come together right in front of you, and that's what happened in Burlington that year. There were things that God had in the works for years, in different people's lives, different churches, in all sorts of different parts of the world—many looking like seemingly unconnected dots on a map. However, all of them finally came to fruition at Burlington in a way that only God can weave together so masterfully. Relationships that were forged decades ago were rekindled and reconnected for the growth of His kingdom; the work we had done for those first few weeks was already producing fruit.

Take Clint, for example. Clint was the meanest guy in town, and got saved early on during the Burlington Revival. But the aftermath of that was pretty exciting too—a story that we only learned about several days later. Little did we know that Clint's presence wasn't just about us impacting Clint's life; as it turns out, what started as a burden we had for him later turned around and became a burden he actually lifted from us. Clint owned a Verizon store, and he is the reason we were able to live stream services as each night grew larger and larger—because he gave us free internet to do so. Out of one man's obedience to the calling of the cross, within days hundreds more were impacted directly because of the work of that new believer in Christ's hands. Only God can do that.

In speaking about God putting the pieces together, I would be remiss if I did not mention what we call *the team*. Years ago, God began developing relationships and bonding our hearts together. Just a bunch of young kids fresh out of Bible college, with hearts to do something for the Lord. While I was on staff at Victory, I met our piano player, Jesse Kragiel. It wasn't long after that Jesse introduced me to Jared Dixon, an evangelist who came to assist with the service, and his family. A few years later, a young man named Heath came to Bible college at Victory, and we became friends. All of these people now are a major and integral part of what we do. The list goes on and on, but sovereign in detail that God put all our hearts together. Each has their own busy ministry, but we all come together for big events and crusades throughout the year. Among us, there is never a hint of jealousy or politics, choosing instead to remain of one mind and one accord, with one united goal of preaching the Gospel to as many people as we possibly can. Jesse still plays the piano, Jared leads the music (and is incredible at running or moderating a service), and Heath does an incredible job organizing and bringing structure to what we do. Each of these men of God are my friends, and I am forever grateful for the opportunity to serve the Lord with them.

I also am grateful for my Pastor and mentor, Dr. Ralph Sexton, Jr., and the incredible role he would eventually play at Burlington, one that none of us could have foreseen. When Brother Heath first came up in the ministry, he went out to work for Pastor Sexton, who ran tent meetings throughout the 1980s. Through that work, Brother Heath ended up learning how to put up the tent, and push pitchforks around for Pastor Sexton's tent ministry. During that time, he met Daniel Buchanan, who for years had prayed at Pastor Sexton's meetings. Brother Randy's wife, Mrs. Lisa, played the piano for some of Pastor Sexton's meetings in the 1980s, as well.

For me personally, Ralph Sexton was always a hero of mine. He had always been an encouragement to me. But in 2012, exhausted from evangelism, and in a very low place for us both, Becky and I were asked by Pastor Sexton to come to Trinity in Asheville and take a full-time position as one of his assistants. This was an amazing opportunity for us, and one that we jumped on. It was there that I had the chance to be mentored by Pastor Sexton, and through his ministry God birthed a burden in my heart for revival. Looking back, it is amazing how God put all these pieces together.

When we ran out of space in the church, and were trying to figure out where to go, you could see even more of God's hand at work. Pastor Sexton had never let anybody use his tent before—with good reason, because it's so expensive to manage—so we knew that it was a long shot to begin with. But Brother Hobbs agreed to call Pastor Sexton and, instead of saying no, he said that not only would he let us borrow it, but that he wouldn't charge us a dime to do so, as long as we agreed to take up an offering for his ministry one night during the week. Through all those seemingly convoluted, unrelated relationships, God connected Pastor Sexton and me to the point that when I needed something, he was there to supply the need. Only God could do that, and to God be the Glory!

There we were, armed with this huge, thirty-five-hundred-seat tent—with one problem we hadn't thought through at that point. Where in the world—let alone in Burlington, North Carolina—can you put a tent this big? We'd need a full twenty acres to put it up and park cars around it, at least. Where could we possibly find that much space in such a short amount of time, on the cheap?

THE PROMISED LAND

Enter Don Cox, a Presbyterian businessman, who lived in the area and owned Cox Toyota, right off of exit 140, and just so happened to have a large parcel of land that sat right beside his dealership. After hearing the story of what God was doing there, Mr. Cox not only was generous enough to make the property available to us, but he donated the property to us to use the entire time at no charge. There's no telling how much that would have cost us if we had to lease it. In fact, while he would be too humble to share this, I asked for permission to also share that he paid the electric bill for those seven or eight weeks in the tent, and advertised the revival at his expense on a digital billboard that sits just over the dealership. That week, he even sacrificed new sales opportunities to let us use his prime location signage to advertise the revival.

I'll always remember seeing Mr. Cox sitting on that front row, and as people would get saved and we'd line them up in front of the stage, and he'd stand there watching, the new converts right in front of him, with smiles and tears. He later told us that it was one of the greatest joys of his life to walk down that aisle, giving each new convert a brand-new Gideon Bible.

During those days I remember the pressure and anxiety of thinking, "What are we going to do now?" "How are we going to make this happen?" All those questions flooded our minds constantly. But I also remember a phrase that I said out loud that pushed me through adversity and fear, and that was this. "I would rather give it our best shot, and fail, than look back the rest of our lives and wonder what God would have done." In retrospect, it was so silly to worry about anything. God met every need, and in fact, He usually did it before we knew we needed it. At Burlington, we continued to say, day by day, that we wanted God to do something that no man could take credit for. It had become our unwritten mantra, so to speak, for the revival. And because of these incredible connections that God had made throughout the years, and the things that He did at that time, there's not one man today among us that can say or has said, "Because we did this, it happened." It was God over us, God around us, God in us, God through us, and God through so many other people, as well.

Mr. Cox shared his perspective with me:

I had met Brother Randy a few months before the revival started, at an Easter Pageant. I attend Northside Presbyterian Church but I was interested in going anywhere, to support any denomination that forcefully preaches the Gospel. I hadn't heard much about the revival when I received a call from Pastor Hobbs in May. He told me that they had been having revival here at our church and had run out of space. At that point in time, they were thinking about getting a tent and so Pastor Hobbs was calling to see if they could put it up on our property on Danville Road, which sits just off the interstate on a frontage road.

From a business perspective, it crowded the street we were on. For any other event I would've had significant issues because of the impact it would've had on our customers, our employees, our reputation and, of course, our business. But the reason I said yes was because I looked at it as a tremendous opportunity to reach the community for Christ. I'm eighty-five years old, and since getting saved, I wanted to do things to reach people for the Gospel, so I viewed this as an opportunity to play a part just by providing this land.

Immediately, good things began to happen. I arranged to have somebody save me a seat on the front row, and so I was able to see things there that I had never seen before. The preaching was so dramatic; the people were so responsive. The Gideons would pass out New Testaments to those who got saved that night, following the services.

There were times that they'd be just getting started and before CT would even have a chance to start his sermons, they would start coming down the aisle.

The anointing and the power of God was so strong, and to witness it first hand was indescribable.

There's been so many repercussions from that decision to simply say, "Yes, Lord, I'll do my part," and I didn't expect (or ask) for any of them, but am grateful for it. Everywhere

I go people still talk about it, and I get feedback even now. One time I got a letter from a lady in Anderson, South Carolina, because her church had made the trip up for the revival and she wanted me to know about it, and shared some kind words. Then there was a card from a family in Illinois. There were buses that came from New York, and Texas, and all over. It truly was one of the biggest revivals ever held in this area, except maybe the Greensboro revival in '51 with Billy Graham. But I've definitely have never seen anything like this since then.

I'm just so pleased that I got to play any part in it at all, and I'm honored that God could use me in it all. When God has done something for you, I feel you have the responsibility to share it, to give Him all the glory, but also to serve as a witness to others who might some day feel like they can have a part to play in the saving of souls, whatever the role might be.

There was plenty more that happened over those days—from the local broadcast media showing us favor, to the state's elected officials, senators and even the Lieutenant Governor of North Carolina coming by to see what was happening. Everyone felt compelled to be a part of it and to witness what God was doing. And it wasn't just about the big names that showed up, either—we probably had over a hundred volunteers that helped every single night, many of which left work at five and drove over to the tent without stopping at home to see their families, or to eat supper. They'd arrive and immediately start parking cars, offering to help anywhere in any way anyone needed, and stayed until eleven at night getting everybody shuttled back to their cars, sometimes even standing out in the worst of rain storms I'd seen in a decade.

There was never a harsh word or a bad attitude. Never a complaint, never a push to get credit, glory, or even paid. All the while, all of them just grateful for being involved.

It was as if God just handpicked us and said, "I'm gonna need you, and you, and I'm gonna need you." No master leadership development plan, no team building consultant, no organized initiative or interviews or man-made process. And by God's grace and sovereignty, we came together and were able to see miracles happen on a daily basis.

It was God, and He alone deserves the glory and praise.

*Pastor Daniel Buchanan led prayer meetings
each morning under the tent.*

TOGETHER
IN PRAYER

To uphold a spirit of prayer, and maintain unity during the revival, Brother Daniel held a morning prayer meeting every morning for all of the pastors who could attend. By the middle of the meeting, there were forty to fifty preachers from out of state who came in— and added to that were not just pastors, but ladies and men from the surrounding Burlington community. Each morning, Pastor Daniel would exhort on the subject of prayer, and then those men would literally gather around those altars in the morning services and pray for protection; that God would save people and revive the churches.

There is no doubt that a lot of the energy and the force of what happened in Burlington began in those morning prayer services. Most successful coaches will tell you that they didn't win their championships during the final game. They'd tell you that the win happened in the weight room; at the training table; in every practice; in the decision to say 'no' to temptations and 'yes' to team curfews; in the decisions each team member made to say 'no' to something that threatened to steal their victory during the season, to say 'yes' to the right choices along the way.

That same way that championship trophies are won or lost, so goes the winning of souls. God is a God of order, and there are things along the way He expects us to set order in the natural, in our preparation, and in our daily habits and commitment to purity and righteous living, so that He can move in the supernatural. We truly felt like the victories that were won at night were actually won in the morning time during those prayers. And those pastors, they were so tired; they had been up until midnight the nights before because of the miraculous late evening services; but they were not going to be denied or deterred. They were committed to doing whatever they could to seeing this common vision come to fruition.

Throughout the mornings of the Burlington revival, God unified us together as leaders, where we could pray the prayer of faith in those morning services. They took me on as a primary burden, realizing that it was critical that I was under the hand of God for my energy, my stamina, my words, my heart, my head, my focus and more. I remember feeling so humbled and honored to slip into the back of the tent and hear those men mentioning my name to the Lord. But in those meetings, prepared for the fight of what was to come that night—there were things we weren't even aware of but that could have popped up and ruined the whole meeting. It was said that we battled at night, but we sharpened our swords in those morning meetings. There wouldn't have been a night of miracles without those mornings; it was all the same. You can't have one without the other and expect God to do the unimaginable, and we had to have it all.

SPIRITUAL WARFARE

During Burlington, Pastor Hobbs once said, "Many churches want revival to come to them, but far fewer of us can actually handle it." The truth is that God has to prepare your church for revival, in part because of the element of spiritual warfare. Any time you seek God's will in something like this, you can be sure that Satan is going to be right there every step of the way—and not just one time at the onset—trying to mess everything up.

For Burlington, there were two primary things that truly prepared us for spiritual warfare: the fifteen years of prayer and preparation, and the constant seeking of God's will in every step that we made, day after day.

I hesitate to share some of this in this book, because Brother Daniel wouldn't want anyone to think we were bragging on him or building him up. However, I feel it is important to give insight into what was the primary element of strength in Burlington... prayer. In fact, *how* he did it was equally as important; many times privately, with no public announcement—just humbly being obedient to God. Every morning, Brother Daniel would lead those pastors in prayer, and every afternoon around four o'clock he and his men would come back secretly and crawl under the platform and start praying. Many nights, he'd have a whole team of men up under that stage praying with him in the exhausting heat.

There were nights when I started preaching and I literally felt like demons had hold of my throat—like I was talking but not talking, and nothing effective was happening. But then I could feel Brother Daniel under that platform praying, and I'd hit another gear. It was like I could feel a wind hit me in the back of the neck, and all of a sudden it was like the windows of heaven were open again. I can't be certain what Moses felt when Aaron lifted his weary arms to keep them help up, but that was the closest I've ever come to understanding. There was something about knowing those men were under me with strength and prayer every moment, lifting me up even through exhaustion, to ensure we would win every battle God intended us to win, despite whatever the enemy had planned.

Honestly, my sermons were the first thing in my mind nearly every day those twelve weeks. The joke about an evangelist is that they've only got five sermons that they just preach everywhere, but the reality is that every morning I'd wake up and say, "Oh God, what am I gonna preach tonight?" It was such a grind, but by the time I'd get into each night's preaching, because of all the leaders who were praying and so many other factors, preaching became like rushing waters of life that I couldn't contain. Preaching was easy in Burlington; I never lost my voice, and God was always faithful to give the message of the night. We prayed for liberty, and God gave us liberty.

When I was in seminary, there was a preacher named Kenny Grant. He said something one time that I had forgotten, but that God used to teach me during Burlington: God can always used a prepared man more effectively than He can use a prepared message. A lot of times we rely on a prepared message so much that we forget this truth. He asks us to be ready in season and out of season, and that He'll bless the things that we set our hands to and prepare a path for us. He's less interested in *what* we prepare, and more interested in *how* we do it; diligently preparing both our message and our hearts to receive from Him and be a conduit for what He needs to happen. He cares less about us being prepared orators, and more about us being prepared men...prepared vessels.

> *"Abide in me, and I in you. As the branch cannot bear fruit of itself, except it abide in the vine; no more can ye, except ye abide in me. I am the vine, ye are the branches: He that abideth in me, and I in him, the same bringeth forth much fruit: for without me ye can do nothing."*
> — John 15:4–5, KJV

Much of being able to decipher God's will does not come from honing our preaching styles or studying to be great theologians. I believe it comes from knowing God, and spending time with Him. My wife Becky would tell you that while I do try my best to read and learn everything I can about being a better husband, I've come to know her better than anyone else because I spend time with her. Sometimes, in fact, we just sit together, blocking out the world, sensing each other's presence as we read, catch up on life and pray together. Through those quiet, intimate times together, a great byproduct is we are preparing our marriage for the storms and battles of life that surely will come that the enemy has in store for us.

Preaching is the same way. Knowing this, I can tell you I was in that little Sunday School room every day of the revival with those Greek lexicons and commentaries and books, reading fifteen chapters a day. I'd take all that stuff down and then just go lay on a mattress in the corner, and talk to God, and listen. Many times I'd just start by recalling what He did the previous night. "God, thank you for saving that girl." "Thank you for saving him." "Let my boy Tucker remember this." "God, let it be so real that Becky and I can't be satisfied with dry old church any more." "God, let this be so real." "Bless the men around me." Before I knew it, the whole day would have passed and I would have just about spent an entire day with Him. And I would walk to that pulpit, and God would just put something there.

I later realized another valuable lesson about preparation and about life. There's something that happens in your prayer life that can produce incredible miracles and move mountains when you begin that prayer time being intentionally thankful versus making requests. When God instructed us in His word to enter His presence with thanksgiving and enter His courts with praise, it wasn't just a cute scripture that we could put to music one day. He was giving us insight into how He responds to us. As a leader, a father, and a husband, I've experienced first-hand how it feels for people to come to me, and before asking me for anything, simply thanking me for things I've already done. When it's not manipulative but authentically thankful for things I've already done, I can't help but respond by wanting to jump in and, figuratively speaking, live in that thankfulness and praise for a bit. That's what God meant when He said He inhabits the praises of His people. When we begin by thanking Him for what He's already done and praising Him, we're literally building a spiritual house for Him to come live in, and inhabit our praise and thanksgiving. Thanksgiving should, for the believer, be more than just an annual holiday. It should be a lifestyle that sets the stage for God to do the impossible.

Throughout those days and weeks, there were some nights that I felt God would not give me anything. On the grounds at the tent, I had a special place that I'd walk to every night, tucked away in the back. Now, I don't know with one hundred percent certainty all the biblical guidelines for what constituted Holy ground, nor could I write a definitive dissertation on it for you to have unwavering guidelines and certainty for every situation of your life you'll ever have to face, but I can tell you this: I know God's voice and I know God's presence, and there was so much praying on that property that when you stepped foot on it, it was undeniably electric, as if a current of the Holy Ghost was charging through it. I would walk on that property and I had one specific pole that I'd go to and kneel down and pray—sometimes it was exuberant and sometimes it wasn't—but no matter how many times I'd kneel there to pray, God would fall on me heavily and would whisper a verse to my heart, changing my plans and disregarding everything I had studied that day. Then I'd get up and walk to that pulpit with that one verse in my heart. The funny thing is, if you went back and listened to that sermon, you'd think someone had written it, planned it, researched it and refined it for three months on that one verse's principle. God had blessed me with words in a way only He can. "Open your mouth and I'll fill it." There were times I wouldn't even leave my prayer pole until it was time for me to walk right up on stage; to make absolutely sure He had given me what He wanted, and to ensure it was all His will, not mine.

In two words, it was pure dependence and obedience. That's what God really wanted out of this whole thing, and not just from me, but from every man and woman out there who were a part of it. There were those who put everything on the line. There were men who were working around the clock. Everyone was fighting their own wars and running on fumes. A lot of preachers don't like things to get out of their control because they feel intimidated, but the biggest thing for me was to say, "Look, I'll admit it. I don't have a clue what's going to happen next, but I'm very aware of what's going on, what God's doing and what we're in the midst of here." And I would remind my group of key leaders daily to continue to be in agreement and of one accord in prayer because I didn't know what I would do if God doesn't do something each day and guide and direct me, and I certainly wasn't about to find out.

Most pastors—and probably me at certain points in time, too— they are so worried about everything being perfect and organized that they organize God out of it. But at that time, everybody was so dependent on God for their part functioning properly as well as working together with all the other moving and changing parts, like a finely-tuned engine. I'm sure there were people out there who thought, "Boy, they are riding high and have this thing all figured out with flawless execution!" But that's part of why we felt it was critical to share as transparently as possible, in this book, as a witness to the truth and to what really happened. Those same people who thought that never knew the things we dealt with behind the scenes. However, I believe it's way less important to try to put up an image of what strong leadership looks like—that would just inflate your perception of us as men. Real power comes from sharing the truth. That way, when you're called to revival—whether it's your family, your church, or your community—you'll know God's pattern and focus less on what you don't know or have, and focus more on what He can do with the two most critical things all believers can bring him: dependence and obedience. He'll take it from there.

I don't want to give the devil power or credit, so it's also a fine line between knowing and believing he's already defeated, and recognizing he's got a plan to try to tear down anything God wants built up. However, the truth about spiritual warfare is that it's a hard road to continually fight the demons coming after what God is trying to do through you every single day. But in 2 Samuel 24: 24, King David talked about how he would not offer anything to the Lord that did not cost him something. I have to agree; every week in Burlington brought challenges, hurdles and opposition, and it all came at a price.

PUTTING STAKES IN THE GROUND

The night we came back to the church and told the people about the pastors' meeting at the Golden Corral was a memory that will never leave me. When we told them about how the pastors unanimously agreed, and the funds were raised immediately, that place went crazy. The excitement was so thick you could cut it with a knife. God was on the move and those people knew it.

With full agreement among all the pastors and community that we would continue the revival meeting under the borrowed tent, and with all the pieces that had come together under God's supernatural power, we all set to work in preparing it. If you've never been part of a team preparing an area for a tent that massive, it's not as simple as just popping some stakes into the ground, as I learned years ago the very first time I was part of helping set one up for someone else. Usually, it takes about two weeks and a lot of moving parts, manpower, and expertise after you've done the grading, run electrical, and prepped the site to then put up the tent. At Burlington, we knew we didn't have that much time, and we worried that the momentum would be lost the longer it took, so we prayed for God to show us a way to do it in only three to four days, and to cover, protect and guide us every step of the way. From where we stood, we didn't have the manpower, the resources, nor the time to pull this off; however, by this time we'd become pretty used to those kinds of odds and had collectively united in our faith that our big God had big vision, big resources, big plans and things already in the works.

We announced to the church that we had the tent and that we would need some help putting it up. Truth be told, I think most of us expected what usually happens when you set up a tent: thirty or forty people show up to help. But that week, another miracle happened. The day we were to start work on the tent site, two hundred and fifty people showed up. People took off work. People just kept showing up. And it wasn't just locals—there were people who had driven hours just to be a part of putting that tent up on that property. I'd never seen anything like it before, and certainly couldn't have planned, coordinated or predicted it.

But the miracles didn't end there. When you have that many people working that fast and that hard, with no prior experience working together, it's not as if you have a well-structured oversight committee and process for checking and rechecking every part to ensure everything is done correctly. Not only did we need God to pull off the miraculous for tasks we were aware of, but we also needed Him for problems we weren't able to predict. The truth is, people aren't perfect, and we make mistakes. But that's why God promised us that His mercies are new every morning. When you have new mistakes every day, He has new mercy awaiting!

God covered us from our own mistakes and other unexpected challenges the whole time. For instance, initially in our rush to get two hundred and fifty volunteers mobilized and the tent put up, we set the tent too far away from the power source—a mistake that typically takes about two months to get fixed because it involves stopping, waiting, and working with local municipalities to ensure guidelines are established, paperwork is filed and approvals are received and in hand. Fortunately, Heath's father is a lineman for Duke Energy, and after a few calls to explain the situation but also that the work wasn't violating any major areas of concern, his boss confirmed that if he would commit to hanging the meter off the clock, they'd let it slide. So he was able to reset something that would have taken two months in just a day. What an easy-to-overlook example of how we have a great God Who operates outside of time and man-made timelines when He has to accomplish His will.

Finally, the day came where we were going to put the tent up. The trucks arrived, and the whole town was talking about it. There we were, with around two hundred and fifty men, in the heat of June in the South. Heath and other men were leading the charge, directing everyone on what to do and where to go, and despite all the hard work we had to do in the heat of the summer, amidst it all there was an undeniable spirit of pure joy that you could feel more tangibly and real than the heat itself. Everyone was just so thankful to get to be a part of it, and could taste with anticipation the fruit of their labor that awaited.

Hitting a stake into the ground became almost monumental to us that day—it represented the privilege of having a part in this thing. We felt like we were nailing the stakes of the kingdom of God into the ground. None of us had a clue what was about to happen. In our minds, we had rented this tent for a week or two, and we were looking at this moment as a grand finale of what was.

Little did we know it was just the beginning.

In the end, once grading was completed, all the work was done on the site within five days. On the sixth day, we had our usual prayer meeting, and on the seventh day, June 9, 2016, we kicked off under the tent.

LOOKING FOR A SIGN

There is equipment that you can use to speed up some of the work of putting up a tent; for example, there are machines that will drive the spikes into the ground almost immediately, instead of having to hit them repeatedly with a sledgehammer. But there was something about feeling the magnitude of the work we were putting in and the metaphor of driving spiritual stakes into the ground of people's lives, churches and communities that we never would've experienced during the tent setup if we weren't driving them in one by one, by hand. So we opted for manual labor instead. We had been doing that for hours—I've got pictures of us with gloves on, working those things into the ground—when all of a sudden I felt a tap on my back. When I turned around, a man named Brandon was standing there. He was from the sign company, and had stopped by (or so he thought) just to get us to approve the road signs that would lead everyone to the tent site from the interstate.

"Mr. Townsend," he said, "I'm here to show you the road signs design." Looking at him, I could tell in his eyes he was wondering what he had just walked into and onto, but he stayed focused on the task at hand, and gave me the paperwork that included the designs on it. Finally, he said, "What's going on here?"

And I replied, with sweat coming down my forehead and a sledgehammer in my hand, "Man, God's moving over at that church. We've got a thousand people in a building that seats six hundred, God is moving and we are putting up the tent for more space." I kept talking to Brandon, sharing with him how God had given us this tent and how we believed incredible things were about to happen. The whole time I was talking to him, his face was turning white, but I assumed he was amazed at what God had done, and was excited about it. A few minutes later the conversation was over, and before I knew it I was back over that spike, hammering away. It was literally such a quick interchange that I would never have remembered it ever happening, were it not for what happened next.

About an hour later, I'm way further down the site, but I felt that same familiar tap a second time. "Mr. Townsend?" I turned around, and there was Brandon again. This time was different. This time, no words were necessary; I could see it on his face.

"Ever since I left this property, I can't begin to explain what's been going on inside me. My heart's about to beat out of my chest." He told me he wasn't right with God, but that he needed to know how to do it.

And right there, with the tent still laying on the ground, and the stakes sticking up all over, a young man who had come with an assignment to bring us a sign, ironically, gave us a very different sign; another sign that God was able to do exceedingly, abundantly above all we could ask or think through everything we were doing at Burlington. From the preaching to the sweaty pounding of stakes into the ground, it was all righteous work, and it was all capable of being used at any moment by God to drive stakes through the plans of the enemy, through the hard ground of the hearts of Clint and whosoever else would come to that place physically or even online, and bring people into eternal life and relationship with Him.

Brandon fell on his knees. Before I ever preached a sermon; before we ever sung a song; Brandon was on his knees, and I was leading Brandon to God right there on the grass. In that moment, we knew that God was honoring the prayers that had been held over that site, and the prayers that we had prayed for the supernatural to happen, and the prayers that the group at New Hope had prayed for revival all those years. We knew then that we were on to something that was bigger than any revival or tent meeting we'd ever experienced.

Brandon got saved that day, but before he had even left the site, we could hear men all over that property shouting and clapping. Within minutes, as we were rejoicing what God had done for Brandon, three other men had fallen to their knees and gotten saved. I hadn't even preached a sermon yet, and God was already saving people all over that property.

*In the middle of summer heat, capacity crowds
gathered to hear the Word of God.*

A NEW BEGINNING

As we moved into the tent and out of New Hope, we had no idea what to expect. By that time the whole town was talking about the revival. If you went to Walmart, people were talking about the revival in town; if you were on social media, that's what people were talking about. It was a phenomenon, and it was almost too hard to believe. That first night, we set out fifteen hundred chairs, thinking that would cover any extra people we could possibly expect to have picked up over the weekend, but also thinking there was no realistic way we'd need that many chairs.

I'll never forget pulling up to that property that night.

To get to the tent, I had to cross a bridge over the interstate. When I did, I looked around and couldn't believe my eyes. All I could see for as far away as I could see, in both directions, was cars. There were eight lanes on I-40, and even the exit was packed with cars, all trying to get off of the interstate and onto the property. On the frontage road leading toward the tent, every spot was taken, and all I could see was an ocean of steel. Car after car after car.

I remember, to this day, the thought that suddenly gripped me: "Uh oh. That's way more than fifteen hundred people. We're gonna need more chairs."

No one had called me to tell me anything, probably because they thought I might panic, and didn't want me to be distracted from hearing from God and being rested, prepared and prayed up to preach that night. When I saw how many people were flooding in, I realized that up until that point, I had never preached to that many people in one place, in one night, in my whole life.

It was absolute, glorious chaos. There were thousands of people, and no chairs left. Fortunately, Brother Heath and Brother Randy took charge directing ushers and people—they sat the elderly people first, then women and kids, and finally the men, but there were hundreds of men and women that stood all around the back of the tent. Improvising and innovating as best we could, we even took all the cardboard that the chairs were delivered in, cut it up and used it as makeshift seating for all the kids up on the altar that first night.

We had no idea how many people were there the first night, because we didn't even have chairs to count. However, our most accurate guesses of trying to count people in sections and eyeball the spread of the crowd, put it around twenty-three-hundred people or so. What we did get a count of was way more important, though. The very first night, forty-five people walked down the aisle and made decisions for Christ.

There was a significant pivot that first night. In one service, our meeting at New Hope had morphed into a revival across communities. Not just the Burlington community; people drove for hours that night, from churches in Knoxville and Chattanooga, Tennessee, from Marion, North Carolina, and other communities across the region. All these different churches drove in from all over the place—crossing state lines and community lines, and ignoring denominational lines.

"Who hath heard such a thing?

Who hath seen such things?

Shall the earth be made

to bring forth in one day?

Or shall a nation be born at once?

For as soon as Zion travailed,

she brought forth her children."

ISAIAH 66:8

KJV

HOLY GROUND

One of the easiest and most detrimental things that we could have done at that time would have been to try to limit God to the boundaries that we set in place for the revival. It's something that we tend to do—create *rules* of interaction, and boundaries of what we can and can't do in any certain circumstance, and then expect God's sovereignty and Holiness to fit within those, and not go beyond.

This meeting broke all traditions and man-made rules. It refuted every typical excuse like, "We'd like to come, but we've got to get our kids home in bed." Or, "Well, can we work around our own church schedule to coordinate when we can come up?" Or, "Well, anything more than an hour, and we will start to lose people." Let me tell you something: God doesn't need our boundaries, and He won't accept them, either. In fact, I remember a man who called me and was talking about another revival coming up at the time. He said, "Well, brother, we're 50 miles away, but we'll do our best to get over there." And I remember thinking, "If the fire falls, you won't be worried about how far off you are." Because in Burlington, none of that mattered. Distance didn't matter; it wasn't unusual that people would drive two or more hours every day to get there, and would turn around after and drive two or more hours to get back. No one cared that school was in session, or that a service went long, or that there was too much traffic or too many people or not enough seats or that it was too hot. No one cared, because the fire kept falling.

I remember one girl named Olivia, who was graduating from high school with honors, and her graduation was the next night. She came up to me and said, "We can't miss this." Thinking I was giving her the freedom to make a different choice, I empathetically told her to go on and get her diploma and experience her graduation with her classmates. Instead, she looked at me straight-faced and without hesitation said, "Not on your life."

The thing about that tent was that it felt like every one of your senses was alive. You could taste it; you could smell it; you could hear it. It was unbelievable. Even now, when I drive past that tent site, every part of my being comes alive and so many of the miracles and memories are attached, and so many others who were there have said the same thing to me since then.

During those three months, it was hard to describe, but it was almost like you were afraid to miss a single second there. When you woke up in the morning, you would know "I need to get such-and-such done at the church…or with family…or with my kids…but I've got to get it all done because the prayer meeting is at ten in the morning." And it wasn't the usual Sunday School mentality, where you *have* to be there on time for Sunday School and feel the pressure of the obligation. It was more like a compelling draw—a feeling that, if I'm not there at ten, I am going to miss the miraculous. I have to be there. The verse that I'm reminded of as I think about this is found in Isaiah:

> *"Who hath heard such a thing? Who hath seen such things? Shall the earth be made to bring forth in one day? Or shall a nation be born at once? For as soon as Zion travailed, she brought forth her children."*
> — Isaiah 66:8, KJV

That's really what happened. People got to the place, like Zion, where they said "I'd rather die and never make another dollar, just for my children to be saved or just to see and experience God. I'm tired of the devil messing with my family and my community; I'm tired of the destruction." And when people started praying like that, and when that tent went up and all that prayer ensued, it was like the womb of the church had opened back up. God was pleased; the requirements had been met. People say it was a God thing, which it absolutely was. But we had a decision to make as far as the part we were going to play, and a question to ask: Are we going to limit God, or not?

After accepting Christ as his Savior, Jesse Hursey shared the Gospel with others at the altars under the tent.

THE LOST ARE FOUND
By Jesse Hursey

Jesse Hursey is a young man that was saved at the Burlington Revival, under the tent. His family owns the Hursey's BBQ restaurants in that part of the country. (On a side note, their food is amazing!) Jesse has a wonderful testimony, and is still doing well; an active member of Pastor Hobbs' church and has been called to preach. Instead of me telling you his story, I thought it would be better for you to hear it directly from him. Here is what Jesse had to say about how God changed his life at the Burlington meeting.

I live on Hwy 40 where the tent was, but I work east of the tent, so I never drove by it. I never saw it until one day, a lady at work asked if I had heard about the revival in town. I told her I hadn't. Truth was, I didn't know anything about it. I went home that afternoon like usual, but I couldn't get the word "revival" out of my mind. I don't tell many people this, but before I even went to that meeting, I couldn't watch TV that afternoon; I tried to drink an alcoholic beverage and I remember not even being able to taste it. And at that point, I hadn't even been to the meeting.

Now, I know that a sinner's a sinner, but I was in a very deep, dark place at that time, and somehow, just by the aggravation of the word "revival" in my mind, I decided to go to this thing. Little did I know what I was running into and how it would forever change the trajectory of my life.

I pulled up into that lot, and I didn't even know what a revival was—the church I grew up in never had one. All I saw was a huge tent and a lot of cars, and I probably walked a half mile just to get to this thing, not even knowing what I was entering into at the time. Inside that tent, I saw nothing but sawdust shavings, metal chairs and a piano. Somehow, I was able to find a seat, but I remember looking back and seeing the back side of the tent, and so many rows of people standing everywhere. The atmosphere in the tent was electric. You could taste the air.

I remember sitting down in that tent, and a man beginning to pray. I had my head bowed, and I can't even describe what happened to me when that man started praying—it rocked me. Here was a man that had a boldness on him that I had never before experienced from anything the world had to offer; I had met some of the most well-known people around the region because of my family's standing in the community, but I had never seen the kind of boldness that was on this man. And in this boldness, he declared that God was real, that Heaven was real, and we are all gonna die one day and that there really is a man named Jesus.

I really liked going to the meeting, so I'd eventually come back and bring people with me to fill up chairs under that tent. I liked it so much that I felt compelled to bring friends with me. Night after night I would bring co-workers, friends and family and nearly every night they would walk down the aisle and trust Christ. But something was missing in my life. I went to the preacher—Brother CT—and told him, "I've been bringing all these people, but I honestly can't tell you a time I was actually saved. I don't even know if I'm a Christian." I think he knew that God was dealing with me, but he told me, "Jesse, I can't tell you if you're saved or lost, only you and God know that. I don't want you to be confused, but I want you to go home and pray about it, that God will show you if you're lost, or saved."

Let me tell you: that was the worst night of my life. God showed me I was lost on the side of that highway, on the side of that tent. And I saw myself lost in the eyes of a Holy God; disconnected from Him. Throughout my entire life up to that point, there had never been a power greater that could show me that. I couldn't show it to myself, and nobody else could do it for me. That night, I tried to sleep and I couldn't. I felt like I was about to die; my heart felt like it was beating out of my chest, and God showed me I was lost. I went to work the next day, and people must've thought I was coming in high, or strung out, from the night before. I had worked at our family-owned BBQ restaurant for years, and that day I couldn't even make a BBQ sandwich. About two o'clock that afternoon, I decided that I had to make things right.

I guess at that point, the only confidence I had in anything I was thinking or feeling came when I was in that tent, so I made a beeline for it. I was driving so fast to get there that my car made a huge commotion sliding in on the gravel driveway. I ran into that tent where Brother CT and many of the other pastors and volunteers were setting up chairs, and I told him, "I'm lost. I can't wait until tonight; I gotta get saved right now." And right there, on that altar, in my red Hursey's BBQ work uniform, I fell to my knees on that altar and asked Jesus to save me. Life has never been the same since.

Looking back, I believe God was peeling each layer off that the devil had on me, and was building in me the faith to place my trust in Him. Once I came up off that altar and the transaction was made and my soul was redeemed, it was the craziest thing—I was now introduced to this spiritual world for the first time in my life. Today, I no longer feel the need for money or material things to be happy in life, and I certainly don't need all that the world has to offer. The power was real, and is to this day. The changes are permanent, and God gets all the glory.

A MOTHER'S FAITH

One night, after the service, I was out walking around the tent and I saw a lady over near the altar weeping. Becky and I went over to her to ask what was wrong, and she ended up openly expressing the fact that she was having a hard time. She talked about seeing all these people getting saved, and how to her, each of those people represented someone's son or a daughter getting saved. She was struggling with her faith, and admittedly a little bit of jealousy, because she had been praying for her own son to get saved for years. In her mind, she was seeing God save other people's sons and daughters and was so grateful for it and happy for those moms and dads, but still grieving over her son, who was lost and living in Tampa, Florida. After talking a bit, we agreed together, and we prayed for her son and for his salvation. We got his name, and told her that we would continue to be in agreement with her, and pray for her and for her son, and specifically that God would save her son.

In Mark 2, there is a story about the man who was paralyzed, who couldn't come to Jesus. But their faith was so strong that his friends not only took him to see Jesus, but they ripped up a roof just so they could get their friend close to the Son of God.

> *"When Jesus saw their faith, he said unto the sick*
> *of the palsy, Son, thy sins be forgiven thee."*
> — Mark 2:5, KJV

In this story, when someone was brought by faith to Jesus, He not only had the power to heal, but to save.

One night as I walked on the platform, Heath stopped me. I could tell he was excited. He said, "You are not going to believe this," as he pointed to the left side of the tent. There she was, the same lady that was so burdened for her son. I didn't understand, so I asked, "Heath, I'm glad she is here, but she's been here a lot, so what's the big deal?"

He quickly pointed out to me that it wasn't her he was pointing out, but who was seated beside her. There he was, her son, under the tent with her. Heath began gently pulling me off the stage saying, "You have got to know this story before you preach tonight!" Heath began to tell me about how burdened and full of faith that mother was as she left the tent nights earlier, when we all agreed and prayed together. He began to tell me the story of how she went home, and by faith she went online and bought a plane ticket from Tampa to Raleigh for her son. She then called him, and told him she wanted to see him, and had bought him a plane ticket to come visit. He gave her all kinds of excuses of why it wasn't a good time for him, but she was persistent, so he agreed. Her son thought, at that point, that he was just headed for a weekend visit with his mom. That day, she picked him up at the airport, and they headed to get something to eat. When they finished their meal and catching up, they got back in the car and she started driving. As he asked where they were headed next, without lying, she let him know there was an event in town she'd wanted to take him to for a little while. "It is going to be wonderful, you'll see."

They parked in an overflow lot, and got on the shuttle. Needless to say, when they arrived at the tent, he wasn't the happiest traveler that day, once he realized his momma had brought him to a revival. "Momma, you brought me to church, haven't you?" She smiled and took her usual seat under the tent.

Heath and I got on our knees and began to pray. I asked the Lord that night, "Lord, if you have ever filled me, please fill me tonight. Lord, if you've ever preached through me, preach through me tonight, but Lord, please don't disappoint that poor little momma's prayer!" Later, as I was preaching, I looked back towards the area they were sitting, and I caught a glimpse of him out of the corner of my eye. He was already sitting on that folding chair with his arms tightly crossed, not wanting to hear anything I had to say. He wore his Tampa Bay hat cocked sideways with flip flops and a tattered pair of shorts. It wasn't tough to notice how mad he was; he did not want to be there.

But there is something so very powerful about the power of the Word of God. It's not a man's intellect, education or charisma that gets the job done; it is the power of the Gospel (Romans 1:16). Somewhere in the middle of that preaching, he broke. I watched as his arms unfold, as he inched up on the edge of his seat and began to hang on every word I said. Suddenly, he began weeping. When the invitation came, he was clinging tightly to the back of the chair in front of him. His momma was praying as other people began to make their own way down the aisles, but he still wouldn't budge. However, a little while later, as we were singing a song of invitation, I was looking through the crowd when I saw a beautiful sight. There it was, a woman's fist going up in the air, as if she's jumping up and down. All I could make out was that little wrist going up in the air, and initially I wondered what was going on, not making the connection until moments later, as I'm looking through the crowd, and there he was. Her son—for whom we'd all been in agreement for and prayed about—making his way forward. Here comes her boy. He's broken. He's got his head hung down, and he's walking towards the front. As they brought him past me, I heard him calling out to God, and he literally fell on that altar.

All I remember hearing next was his momma behind him, shouting, "God saved my boy! God heard my prayer!" all the way back to her seat. She shouted the rest of that night, and all the way back to her car. When she couldn't figure out how to get Jesus to her boy, she brought her boy to Jesus. Her simple act of faith—buying a plane ticket for her son—changed both of their lives, forever.

THE KING HAS ONE MORE MOVE

During the revival, there were stories every night of men and women and children who were falling on their faces before God. Some of these stories came through the testimonies of others, that we as a leadership group never witnessed first-hand; we simply heard about them later on as the community recounted them to each other, and to us. One of these such stories was about the daughter of a local college professor; I'll simply share the story as it was told to me.

This professor was known for his firm atheistic views, but he later published a post regarding his daughter's experience with the revival. In it, he essentially said, "You all know what I believe, but I think it's interesting to hear this from my daughter's perspective about the revival going on in Burlington."

What followed was an account of the daughter's testimony of coming to Burlington. In it, she talked about driving by the tent on a daily basis, where at first, she thought the dealership had a big car show going on. When she heard that it was a revival in town, one of the statements she made early on in the post really got me. She said, summarily, "I could not deny the fact that every time I would drive by, something in my heart would pull me to see what was going on in that tent." She kept telling herself that, if it was there tomorrow, she would go. Then, it turned into, "If it's there next week, I'll go." Every time she went back to check, it was still there.

One night driving back home after a workout at the gym, she looked over at the tent and all the cars all along that frontage road. That night, she resolved, "I'm going tonight." When she got close, there was nowhere to park, so she just pulled into the driveway, right in the middle. She didn't think she'd end up there for long, so she stood at the back of the tent in her gym clothes just watching, curious to see what was going on. She described what she saw; a young preacher up there preaching about the love of Jesus, and about how no matter who you are, or what you've done, He loves you and can change your life. For the first time in her life, she said, she heard and understood the gospel of Jesus Christ. And then, she shared something I'll never forget. She wrote about how the preacher began to ask people to come toward him and accept Christ as their Savior. She said, "Believe it or not, the next thing I knew, I found myself walking down that aisle in my gym clothes, and kneeling at that wooden altar, and a lady I'd never met brought over a Bible to show me how to be saved. That night on my knees, I called on the name of Jesus and asked Him to forgive me of my sins and to save me. I still don't understand it all, but I slept better last night than I ever have, and I've got peace like never before."

Another story that is dear to my heart happened during one of the weeks we were under the tent. By this time, God had transformed that tent into a soul-saving station. There was a unified effort by the surrounding churches to get as many unsaved people under the sound of the Gospel as possible. Pastor Brad Williams of Wayside Baptist Church in Hillsborough, North Carolina, was very involved in doing just that. He was faithful to bus people from his community to the tent, and one of the men he brought was named Darnell. Darnell was a tall, strong, African-American man who at first glance didn't seem to want anything to do with that tent. It's still a mystery to me how they convinced him to come, but the first night he arrived, he absolutely refused to go inside. However, the very next night, there he was on the bus again, on the way to the revival. That night, he at least sat under the tent, but remained stone cold. Pastor Williams testified that he went over to Darnell to spend some time with him and share with him the love of Christ. The next night, Pastor Williams was not able to make it to the revival, but the bus went on without him. Once again, there was Darnell on that bus.

That night I preached, and I felt like I gave it everything I had. I was soaking wet all the way down to my socks. (You try preaching in a suit and tie, in ninety to one hundred degree weather.) That night, the altar space was full of altar workers, helping those that came forward for salvation. As I scanned the altars I noticed a big man off to my left (who I would later know to be Darnell). A few of our altar workers approached him, but then left him abruptly. For a moment, I got nervous, but had to stay focused on preaching. Still, it was unnerving. All of these things flew through my mind: Why is this guy here? Why is he staring at the people on the altar? Is he a threat to people under the tent? While Jared was singing, "Why Not Tonight," I walked down to where he was, approached him, and reached out to shake his hand. He never acknowledged it, and kept his hands firmly by his sides. I smiled and said, "Hello sir, what is your name?" To which he responded, "None of your business!"

Not what I expected. I made a few more attempts to help him, but eventually walked away as he wouldn't even talk to me. Security was quick to keep their eyes on him, as we had no clue what was going on with that man, and we always err on the side of caution.

The next night was Friday night. Typically, Friday nights were our largest crowds. People would drive in from hours away, and that night we probably had four thousand people under the tent. I preached a sermon entitled "The King Has One More Move." After preaching from the text of Elisha and how he was surrounded in 2 Kings 6, my final illustration was about an intriguing painting that was once displayed at the Louvre art museum in France called *Checkmate*, painted by Friedrich Moritz August Retzsch. I had read this illustration in a book years prior, and had shared it many times. This painting was to portray the game of chess and the concept of checkmate. If you're not familiar with chess, checkmate occurs when a player's king is surrounded, has no options to escape, checkmate is declared and the game is over.

The story behind the painting is about how, one day, a chess master went to the museum to view this famous painting. He gazed at the painting for what seemed an eternity, examining the art, but also thinking through every possible move on the board. Suddenly, the chess master began to yell, his voice bellowing through the halls of that museum, demanding the painting be taken down, declaring, "It's not checkmate; the king has one more move!" The game that was declared over was not over, for one reason: the king still had one more move— one more way of escaping death that no one else could foresee.

That night we dramatized that story, comparing and contrasting everyday life with this checkmate painting. We positioned one man on stage as if he was playing chess with the devil. The devil was dressed out to look like you might imagine the devil depicted, and I taught about how he throws all the vices of this world at this man, in an attempt to get him to make wrong moves. The devil will offer anything he can think of to ruin this man's life. One by one, different sets of actors walked on stage offering the man choices like drugs, alcohol, women, and more. With every wrong move, the chess pieces were positioned perfectly by Satan, surrounding the man. Defeated, the man fell to his feet as the devil placed a gun in the man's hand and suggested he end it all. With gun in hand, the devil stands above him and yells, "Checkmate!"

Just then, out of nowhere, our actor portraying Jesus descended on the dramatization and went straight to the chess board. The devil began to tremble, pointing his finger at the man, claiming him, shouting, "He is mine!" Piece by piece, Jesus kicked away the chess pieces surrounding the man, and they all fell off the stage. The devil ran off the stage, out of the tent and by that point, people under the tent were on their feet. Jesus then knelt down and took care of the man. He took away the gun that had been placed in his hands, cleaned him off and helped him stand to his feet. The man embraced Jesus, as I began to preach:

> "It's not over until God says it's over. The King has one
> more move! The King has one more move!"

That night, one by one, a stream of people began walking down the aisle under conviction to be saved. I remember calling for more altar workers at one point, there were so many coming forward. After some time went by, I began to scan the crowd, as people were on those old half-log altars, calling on the name of the Lord. That was when I noticed a group of men shouting over in the corner.

There was Darnell, piled up on that altar giving his heart to Christ. When I walked up to him, his demeanor was completely different as he looked me in the eyes, and a big smile came over his face. He knew the power of the devil declaring checkmate over his life, but now he also knew the power of Christ setting him free.

At the time we wrote this book, we called Pastor Williams about Darnell. With great joy, Pastor Williams shared with us about Darnell getting baptized, joining the church and even singing in the choir. He told us what a joy he is and the dramatic change that Jesus made in his life. Darnell's story reminds me how thankful I am for the life-changing power of the Gospel. No matter how far gone, no matter how down-and-out, no matter where they've been or what they've done, Jesus has never met a sinner he couldn't save.

The King always has one more move.

WHERE DOES THE HATE COME FROM?

The Burlington Revival had continued through May and June, and as we rolled into July the meeting was in full swing. Even in the scorching heat of a Southern summer, capacity crowds filled the tent each night. Scores of people were being saved nightly, and people were traveling long distances to experience it and see it with their own eyes. It had become a phenomenon on social media, with thousands tuning in live every night.

On Thursday, July 7th, as we all left the tent, we heard the news of the devastating riots and gun fights in Dallas that tragically led to the deaths of five police officers. That night I tossed and turned over the news. I did not know anyone involved personally, but it bothered me to my core. I couldn't sleep, so I got up and it was quickly evident that the Lord was working something in my heart. I opened my Bible and began a study on hate. After studying for a while, I knew my assignment for the next night. I felt led to publicly address the Dallas shootings, and explain from a Biblical perspective where that kind of hatred came from.

The next morning, we announced on social media that I would be talking about the shootings that took place in Dallas. Everyone was talking about it; the shootings were all over the news. The media caught word of what I would be preaching that night, and as I arrived at the tent, I suddenly faced multiple news agencies with their cameras pointed directly at the pulpit. People who had never been to the tent came that night, wondering what I was going to say. Would I take the side of the police? Would I take the side of those who felt injustice? The nation was divided, and in the midst of such a racially charged climate, the tent was packed—some out of curiosity, some to hear how I'd handle it, and others desperately looking to make some kind of sense out of the tragic events. The pressure that night was evident. There wasn't much singing that night at all; Jared sang a few congregational songs, and I went straight to the pulpit.

With news cameras rolling, I asked everyone to open their Bibles to two places. One was in the book of Genesis, the other in the book of Revelation. I introduced the message by talking about the shootings and tragic loss of life in Dallas, events driven by a hate so divisive it can tear us from our fellow man, turn us against each other, driving us to hate those on the other side of our own racial, socioeconomic, spiritual and cultural lines.

I asked everyone to consider where they thought that kind of hate could come from. How can two people who could have easily found themselves playing together on the same playground as kids, grow up with two very different views on life, and grow to hate each other as a result, without even knowing the other's name.

While I suspect the crowds came thinking they would receive a politically-motivated speech and my personal views on the subject, God gave me a boldness and a liberty to run straight to the Gospel. We looked in the book of Genesis and saw where hate began, in the heart of Satan. I shared how sin, hate and pride had been fueled in the heart of mankind since the beginning. At the root of man's problem you won't find a gun problem or a racial problem; at the heart of mankind, you'll find that man has a sin problem, and Satan himself is the puppet master behind the curtain, pulling the strings. While we hate each other and become even more divided, the devil stands in the corner laughing as we fall into his master plan.

"What are we to do with this sin problem? I am glad you asked."

That night, with cameras running, a full tent, elected officials and all, I had the privilege of sharing the greatest truth of all time, about how Jesus came to this world to seek and save that which was lost. I shared how He came to put away sin by the sacrifice of Himself and that He was born to die. I explained how Jesus lived thirty-three perfect sinless years; He never had a bad thought, never did anyone wrong and how He was the spotless Lamb of God, slain before the foundations of the world. He was a miracle worker, a healer, a deliverer and the fulfillment of prophecy. He was the Son of God. They lied about Him, conspired against Him, arrested Him, beat Him, scourged Him, spit upon Him and then nailed Him to the cross.

You could hear a pin drop, and I knew God wanted me to press on, so I did, unabashedly. I described how, after those long, lonely hours on the cross, they gave Him vinegar to drink, mocked Him and laughed at Him, but how they could not kill Him because He willingly gave up His life. I shared John 3:16, with cameras still rolling.

At any time, I explained, Jesus could have called ten thousand angels to rescue Him off the cross, but He stayed there, freeing mankind from the penalty of sin while the wrath of God was poured upon Him that day as He took upon Himself the sins of the whole world. "What a Savior!" I preached, telling them how Jesus cried, "It is finished" and gave up the ghost, and how all of hell began to party, believing that they had defeated God's redemption plan. By this time, as we say in the church, *we were havin' church!* People were on their feet and there was a heavenly roar under that tent, as I went on to preach how, about that time hell was partying, there was a knock at the door and the demons' knees began to tremble, as they looked through the keyhole and there He stood, the one they thought they'd defeated. Jesus took the keys to death, hell and the grave, and on that third and glorious morning, Jesus got up by His own power, and is alive forever more!

I had dealt with where hate came from, how it was defeated, and so I finished by explaining when it would end. I turned to the book of Revelation to that final battle, as Satan in all of his pride really feels as if he would defeat God, and read about how fire falls from heaven and devours them in that great battle. I preached about how the battle is described as being so intense that the blood will be as deep as the bridle on a horse. I asked them if they wanted to know when the hate would end, and as they began to shout yes, so we went to Revelation:

> *"And the devil that deceived them was cast into the lake of fire and brimstone, where the beast and the false prophet are, and shall be tormented day and night for ever and ever."*
> — Revelation 20:10, KJV

I taught about how, at that exact moment, we will be rid of all hatred, and the mastermind behind it all will be defeated by God and thrown into the Lake of Fire. That one that causes so much division…that one that conspired between you and your family… that one who addicted your kids to drugs—his days are numbered.

As the invitation was given that night, scores of people walked the aisle to put their faith and trust in Christ, and with the media outlets putting it all over television, there's no telling how many people heard the Gospel that night. "For whosoever shall call upon the name of the Lord shall be saved." (Romans 10:13, KJV). What a night, and what a Savior!

Before I end this chapter, I feel like I'd be remiss in my calling if I didn't stop and ask you a question. After all, if you've made it this far through this book but you're not one hundred percent sure about your eternal salvation, it's no coincidence we're here together at this point. So, I wouldn't be doing what God has called me to do if I didn't ask you the most important question that anyone ever asked me. If you were to die today, are you one hundred percent sure that you would go to heaven? Are things right between you and the Lord? Are you saved? If not, there is no better time than right now to call upon the name of Jesus, and ask Him to save you! And He will, I promise you. But don't take my word for it, take His:

> *"For God so loved the world, that he gave his only begotten Son, that whosoever believeth in him should not perish, but have everlasting life."*
> — John 3:16, KJV

That's it, such a simple scripture, but one that carries with it the promise to secure your eternal future. It was the ultimate gift from God, for you. Will you receive that gift today? I pray you will.

A MIRACULOUS CONVERSION

Sometimes, depending on the history of what a person's been through and the doctrines they've been exposed to, salvation is as much a process of receiving the new as it is unlearning their past. In some cases, people need to get valid questions answered that have plagued them for years, if someone simply takes the time to hear them and answer the questions plaguing their heart. This story is of one such man, a man who had come to the tent a few of nights in a row.

You could tell he was really struggling and troubled, but night after night he would just leave the tent, and then return the next day. A few nights into this pattern, we had a night where we were experiencing really significant breakthrough—that's what we called it when those nights got intense and the altar calls seemed to go on and on—with wave after wave of people coming forward. During that time, a man came down to the altar; it took several people to deal with him, because he had so many questions and just wouldn't let up. Finally, at that altar, he asked the Lord to come into his heart.

I'll never forget going to the pulpit that night and looking at the little card that noted his salvation. On that little piece of paper were these words: "Converted tonight from being a Muslim." I read that card out loud, and that place erupted. Mohammed is still dead, but Christ—Christ is alive.

THE WOUNDS THAT HEALED HERS

Revivals can happen anywhere—churches, tents, coliseums—but the thing about tents is that a lot of times, people who would never set foot in a church will come to a tent. One night, I was preaching on Calvary and specifically, about the wounds of Jesus. As we finished the service, I gave one more altar call. "Look, we're not guaranteed tomorrow; if you're here and you're not saved, come to Christ," I said. "I don't care who you are or where you've been, or what you've done, He will take you just as you are."

Brother Jared Dixon, an evangelist who came on board to help moderate parts of the services and run the music, started singing another verse, and I looked down the middle aisle as this girl came walking toward me. She was dressed in an old t-shirt and short shorts, but what really caught my eye was her skin; I couldn't tell what it was, but her skin looked marked in some way. All over her thighs, her legs, her arms…everywhere.

As she got closer, it was evident that those marks were actually scars from her cutting herself. I'd never seen anybody who had cut themselves that extensively. In my experience, most people who cut themselves try to hide it, but this girl wasn't trying to hide anything—it was almost like she was trying to show it off. And with her colored hair and her piercings all over, it's no wonder she perhaps had never felt like she could walk through the doors of most churches. But there she was, at that tent, hearing about the wounds and cuts of Jesus, and for some reason, it resonated with her. She walked down that aisle that night. When I saw her, I ran to her and said, "What have you come down here for?" Her reply: "Can your Jesus save me, too?"

Of course he can.

A dear saint of God took a Bible, showed her the plan of salvation, and began to deal with this young lady. This girl had such a demonic power in her life, it was like I was living in Mark 5. But when she bowed her head and called on the name of Jesus, I cannot explain to you the victory we felt under that tent. It was deliverance, it was salvation, and the blood of Jesus did it again, proving that there is no person so low He cannot reach! I remember telling her, "It's okay that you came here with scars, because Jesus does, too. But, by His stripes, you are healed."

A NEW GENERATION RISES

When we originally scheduled the tent, we thought we would only need it for about two weeks, so that second Friday night we had scheduled to be Youth Night. This would be a night where churches from across the country who wanted to bring their youth could come. Knowing the history of revival, we understood that anytime anything big happened, at the heart of it you'd find young people who caught fire for God. Our desire was that those young people would come in from all over, and take that burden of revival back to their community.

As we planned this night, we'd also scheduled my good friend and one of the most dynamic preachers of our day—a man out of Washington D.C. named Kenny Baldwin. We brought him in, as well as a singing group called the Rochesters—and went all out for this night. But, as we are feeling most nights at this point, we really didn't know what to expect.

We were afraid because it had been so hot, and to sit out there in that field under the sun would have been unbearable. But God was good to us—a layer of clouds covered the sky for the entire meeting, providing much-needed shade to the almost five thousand people who came that night. The numbers were mind-boggling, and it took us almost an extra hour and a half to accommodate everyone, because the tent was so packed.

As a point of reference, when we first started in the tent, we had planned for fifteen-hundred chairs, and we thought that was ambitious. As those filled up, we went to a local event planner and rented another two thousand chairs—during wedding season, no less. As we planned for Youth Night, we decided to rent another two thousand chairs to prepare for a big surge of people. In the end, as we had more than five thousand people come that night. Our ushers that night worked so hard, pulling chairs from everywhere, while our parking volunteers kept trying to clear the interstate from the back-up of cars waiting to get in. Everything was so much bigger than usual; it was eight o'clock before we got everyone settled and got the meeting started.

The delay was worth it, though. That night was glorious, but it didn't start out that way. The crowd was so massive that I couldn't even see all the way out. To be honest, it was tight as we started. We had learned to expect opposition from hell, especially on this night when so many young lives were at stake. The Rochesters were singing, but there was a noticeable hindrance that night. In my spirit, I began to pray, and so did others. We were praying for breakthrough. All of a sudden a young boy (maybe ten years old), shouting like a seventy-year old man, came running down the middle aisle, weeping and shouting. To some it may have seemed silly, to others even insignificant. But it was so innocent, and it was real. That little boy had tears streaming down his cheeks, running and worshipping God. God used that little boy to break the hindrance on that service. From there, it was on.

Dr. Baldwin got up and preached unlike I had ever heard him before. He preached about the dark days we are living in, and how we desperately need a new generation to rise up and be true blue soldiers of the cross. That man preached the house down. It was electric in that place. I saw something I had never seen that night; nearly a hundred professions of faith, and hundreds of decisions for Christ and full-time Christian service. We announced that night that although we were only scheduled to be under the tent two weeks, that the pastors had agreed that God wasn't done, so we were going to continue.

On a side note, one of the very things we were praying for happened after the youth night. A group of pastors and young people chartered a bus from the Surry County area and fell on the altar, asking to send revival to their community. The next week, Pastor Jonathan Barker and several of the pastors in that area were working together, having their church teen camp. Revival fell there as well. They put a tent up, brought a preacher in and had meeting for many weeks at the same time Burlington was going on. We weren't in competition; we were cheering and encouraging each other on, and praying for each other. Many were saved there, and people in that area are still talking about that meeting!

One thing you can guarantee about fire; it spreads.

It never got old seeing a sinner walk the aisle and accept Christ!

WEATHERING
THE STORM

There are two principles that will forever hold true: In a Christian's walk of faith, there are going to be some rough waters that will test you; and, in the course of twelve weeks in the South in the summertime, there are going to be some big storms.

Under the tent, storms would come up from time to time. Most of the rain and wind we'd experienced really didn't interfere with or threaten what we were doing too much, but, lightening is a different story altogether. If there was lightning, it could shut us down quickly. After all, we were in a giant tent with lightning rods stuck into the ground every ten feet or so; it's not the safest place to be in a thunderstorm, not to mention the concern for liability of that tent collapsing on a thousand or more people. It was something we had to keep a close eye on the whole time, with anxiousness and a lot of prayer.

As much as we are always focused on people and ministry first, there's also a real financial burden that comes with any sort of ministry, and especially one where there was a need for way more resources than we had planned for to accommodate way more people than we ever knew to expect. So as a revival like this takes on a life of its own, the ability to receive an offering as new people come becomes more and more critical to financial survival. If you run out of money, you run out of a lot of options to continue God's work. Financially, to get shut down by a storm—even for just one night—could have been devastating. Think of it this way: on Wednesdays, we took up an offering for Brother Ralph, for letting us use the tent, and Friday we didn't take up an offering. So all of our budget—about nine thousand dollars—had to be covered by Monday, Tuesday and Thursday night offerings. So when the storm would come in, we would panic, because how else would we make that money up?

We should have grown accustomed by that point to expecting God to provide, and it wasn't that we didn't still believe it. But, we're also human, and I have to admit that there was real anxiety around these storms because of that, let alone the idea of God's miraculous revival becoming a media frenzy and take a horrible turn for the worse if something awful were to happen due to weather. But God was always in control, no matter what was brewing in the skies.

One night, a storm came in and the policeman called for us to get everyone out. He made his way up to the pulpit and declared, "We need you to go to your cars for about thirty minutes." The whole time I remember thinking, "Well, you've ruined it now; they're all going home." Quite frankly, I wouldn't have blamed them. But when that storm ended a while later, I promise there were more people that came back in than had left in the first place. I remember praising God and being so thankful, but also chuckling inside thinking that any other time, if a church had their air conditioning go two degrees off, they would lose people left and right.

God continued to amaze us through all the storms. There was even another night where a storm edged up on the tent, and we kept waiting for it to hit, but it never did. When we went back to look at the radar, that same storm had literally split in half just before it hit us, and completely missed the tent altogether. In fact, one of the local meteorologists from a local television station commented about this and referenced it as a miracle!

There was one night, though, where the storm of all storms rolled in, and it was one that none of us will ever forget as long as we live. We were in the tent, with it packed full of people, when out of nowhere a storm came up. It wasn't on the radar, but it began blowing and moving some of the ground poles. We considered stopping the service, and one of the leaders came up to me, and asked if we should shut the service down, but that storm was so violent that by the time it hit us, the men were scrambling to lower the walls of the tent, and the officials decided we were safer under the tent than outside. When they went back to check the radar and make some calls to find out what they could from the various weather reports, they got word out of Greensboro nearby that this storm was not only coming, but it was qualifying at a level barely under being labeled an official tornado. As we weighed heavily and wrestled with what to do, the wind began to pick up, blowing underneath the tent and turning it into a big air balloon. In retrospect, it might've been the best thing that happened, because we were suddenly out of time to think about a decision, and had to simply react.

Some of the key men went to Brother Daniel and said "We need to pray," and Daniel looked right back at them and said, "We've prayed; God heard, and He is in complete control!"

The weather grew harsher and harsher, and panic picked up. I continued trying to tell people that everything would be fine, but I honestly didn't know for sure, other than I knew God was among us and over everything. At this point, the numbers of attendees had grown so significantly that there was no way to get them all out safely, so our only option was to hunker down and hold through it, together, in that tent. Still, we were ultimately going to be held accountable for that decision as well as for the well-being of almost four thousand people, who were essentially stuck in a grounded hot air balloon in sixty mile-per-hour winds.

In the thick of it, the poles of the tent started picking up in the wind, so people started trying to grab them and hold them down, to try and keep the tent from flying away. Remember, we're in a tent, in a tornado; lighting is striking and people are grabbing metal poles. What were they thinking?

Water began rushing in over my head through the tent, and I became very aware that I had to look calm, because if I appeared panicked, pandemonium might quickly ensue and people would surely get hurt. The tent was rocking; it was billowing in the middle, and I was scared to death. I look around and there were prayer warriors getting on their knees. At some point shortly thereafter... the storm stopped.

At my core, I just wanted to go home. I think everybody there was exhausted by the stress of it all. I walked up to the pulpit and just spoke the few words I could think of that hit me as I approached the pulpit. "You know, God doesn't do anything by accident. What if this storm had blown this tent off, and a pole hit you in the head, and you died? Would you have gone to heaven or to hell?"

That's all I said. I didn't preach a sermon; I hadn't taught a thing. But that very second, sixteen people walked down the aisle to that altar to get saved.

I remember one specific girl who walked down the aisle that day. She was cut up all over her wrists, and you could tell she had just lived an incredibly difficult life. I remember her that day, walking down that aisle with her shoulders slumped, broken. She fell on that altar and I heard her calling out to Jesus. "Jesus, please forgive me."

Would she have ever gotten saved if that storm hadn't blown in there? I don't know the answer to that; but I know that on that day, after that storm, she did.

The truth is, as scary as all that was, there are people there who may never have given their life to God had they not been confronted in a very real way with the reality that, on any given day, they might die. It broke them the way that perhaps no other service could have, and I realized that God had us exactly where He wanted us.

Teens gathered in Gatlinburg, Tennessee for the annual Carolina Youth Camp where Burlington Revival was "moved" for one week.

MOVING REVIVAL

Earlier in the year, when we were setting the schedules for our other events, no one ever expected that we would spend twelve weeks in any one place—much less in Burlington. So when it came time for our annual youth camp—which that year was held in Gatlinburg—we really struggled with what to do. We didn't want to unintentionally disrupt what God was doing there, but we were locked in to so many commitments. We gathered together with the pastors and prayed, deciding that for one week, we would "move" the revival to Tennessee, where it would be joined by over one thousand teenagers.

We've always had great youth camps, and most of them in prior years were about rejoicing and excitement, but the depth of life-changing impact, broad scale, had never really been there to the level that we had hoped for. This year, from the very first night, it was totally different than what we had ever experienced before. We had prayed that the same Spirit would transfer from Burlington to Gatlinburg as we preached to those youth, and it did. In fact, one night after the preaching, we witnessed over one hundred people saved.

*Those who made a profession of faith were given
Bibles to help them begin their discipleship.*

AFTER
THE FLOOD

When it was time to go back to Burlington after Youth Camp, I think we all were afraid. We were scared we had broken momentum, or that people would think we weren't committed to what was going on there. Satan doesn't take time off, but he's always ready for an opportunity to cause division. And that last night, as we were preparing to go back, we got a phone call that a massive storm hit, and the whole tent had been flooded out. Back at the tent, sawdust shavings were all washed out, there was standing water, and we didn't know at that time what equipment was damaged or destroyed—everything was uncertain. We found out about the flooding on Saturday, and had to be up and ready to go by Monday. We were told that it would cost over $6,000 to replace all the shavings. We were in a tough spot.

But God's people came together that day. So many people worked around the clock to get everything back in order and fixed up, and miraculously by Monday it was ready for the meeting.

After all that worrying, that Monday night, you would've thought we'd never taken any time off. The same people had returned, and new people had poured in droves once again.

THE PRICE OF LEADERSHIP

To avoid criticism,

Say nothing, do nothing, be nothing.

ARISTOTLE

There's an old adage that you've likely heard a few times in your life: When so many thing are going right, something is bound to go wrong. Akin to Murphy's Law, the same paradigm could also be applied to people, especially when it comes to ministry. The more people prop you up in this life, the higher you are for others to take aim at you.

As the revival continued to be successful, despite the fact that unity was at an all-time high, I would be lying to you if I said everyone was on board. As with anything in life, you aren't going to make everyone happy. I remember some older men of God calling me, as Burlington was at its peak, cautioning me. "Son, hold on, they're about to come after you." I recall thinking, "For what? We're preaching the gospel, people are getting saved, who could find fault or be upset with that?"

Most of the criticism came on social media platforms, online channels and blogs, and they'd spend time verbally tearing down what God was raising up in Burlington. The criticism was widespread in nature, ranging from calling it fake, to accusing us of emotionalism, while others cited all the reasons why the world should dismiss what they were seeing happen in Burlington. The hardest part was that most of them had never set foot there, or come to a meeting. They were just going off what they observed on our live stream, or on our own social media pages, where we unabashedly posted live accounts and didn't stop to worry about filtering through the lens of, "What will people think?" or, "How can we spin this?" We didn't alter anything in any way to fit some preconceived marketing strategy. We were just authentically posting and sharing what God was doing, for His glory; certainly not for ours.

You would think, out of everyone who would attack us for doing God's work in Burlington, that it would be some group of people outside the church, motivated by some underlying political, social or other religious agenda. If you had asked any of us to wager a guess, we would've had a long list in no particular order, ranging in guesswork from groups driven by the homosexual agenda, or the mainstream media, abortion rights activists, atheists, or even the skeptical world in general. But sadly enough, the vast majority of main criticisms came from the 'church'; Pharisees and Sadducees and the religious crowd; hyper-Calvinists who don't believe in altar calls and just believe that everybody who is supposed to get saved gets saved, and who hate what evangelists do to reach people.

I say this not to bring attention to the criticism—in fact, at first I was against putting it in this book at all, and I typically prefer to ignore it and not respond to it. I bring it up because I want to draw out and call out a core principle of revival, or of any move of God where leaders are trying their hardest to be obedient and follow God's leading. When God gives you that kind of vision and you obey and you begin to have any sort of success or momentum, or gain any kind of spiritual traction, there's a price to be paid for following God, and especially for leaders. We talked about spiritual warfare earlier in this book, but I want you to remember this main principle:

That which costs nothing is worth nothing,
and will do nothing.

When you're starting out, everybody loves you. Everybody appreciates you, and they are willing to be there for you. Then, as you begin making a difference, the tables turn and it feels like you're spending less time fighting off demons and more time worrying about the guns of criticism pointed at you from all different angles. If you're not careful or prepared for it to happen, because you believe you're doing God's work and no one would come against that, you're just the kind of target I was, and that the enemy looks for to turn people against.

You can find yourself feeling trapped between the world you know you're called to impact ahead and the community you thought had your back. Any leader who's been in ministry long enough will understand this burden, and if they're being honest and have been in ministry long enough, they'll tell you it can be enough to make you want to stop sometimes. But you can't stop doing God's work, no matter who has something to say. One preacher called me when the criticism started and said, "CT, if you study revival, you won't find one man that was instrumental in a revival that was not highly criticized." So expect it, and remember that the Bible was full of people who God called out so He could do great, unprecedented things through their obedience, and in almost every case, their own family and friends were the ones to turn on them. Just ask Joseph. In fact, Jesus, as you remember, could perform very few miracles in, of all places, the very hometown he grew up in. So take heart. If (or should I say, when) it happens to you, you can take comfort in two pieces of advice I wish I had learned a long time ago.

First, let it be a sign unto you that you must be right in the middle of exactly what God needs you to be doing.

Second, you can't control them, but you can absolutely limit the control they have over you.

Fortunately, there were those who didn't accept the criticism as sound truth. One of those men, Dewey Williams, had heard his friends criticizing me and what was happening in the revival, but couldn't accept it from them without knowing for sure what was going on. So he came to the meeting all the way from Bristol, Tennessee, just to see what it was about. That Friday night, God worked some amazing things in his heart, and he went back and told those men, "You can choose to quit being my friend, or whatever else you want to say or do, but I was there, and that was God, and that was real." Before we knew it, he had gotten with them and connected with Brother Daniel. One thing led to another and soon, he had a huge group of pastors that wanted to do something in Bristol, where we later would plan another revival in 2018, right at the time of the publishing of this book.

Miraculously, just as God did for the three Hebrew children, the fires of criticism did not burn us. Too many people saw it with their own eyes. Too many good men were a part of it. Too many lives were changed. To this day, there are churches that have been bettered by what God did in Burlington. God defended us, and preserved the integrity of what He did in Burlington.

Just as God had taken storms and turned them around for His glory, He'd done the same again, this time with something that all started with one man who had to see and hear something for himself, and when he did realize the truth—there was so much God there that He validated everything. There's nothing any of us could've commented or posted on any social media site that would've had the same impact. Once again, we saw the ripple effect of reaching one key person, and what that impact could have on an entire community of people, even doubters and skeptics of the very work God intended for their good. Sounds a little like the story for the crucifixion, doesn't it? It helps me keep my heart pure and in prayer for people, even those who may today appear to be my enemies, and it comforts me to know that Jesus experienced the same, albeit not on social media.

"The fear of man bringeth a snare: but whoso putteth his trust in the Lord, shall be safe."
— Proverbs 29:25, KJV

"For the preaching of the cross is to them that perish foolishness; but unto us which are saved it is the power of God."

I CORINTHIANS 1:18

THE
REFRESHING
OF GOD

As I'm sure most pastors or evangelists go through at one point or another in their ministry, so many weeks of preaching and running and building and searching God's will had taken a toll on me. I was tired, I was worn out, and I was at such a low point physically and from an energy perspective that I couldn't seem to shake it off. I remember looking at my brothers around me and saying, "Boys, God's got to do something for me: I've done all I can."

I was exhausted. Not just really tired; I'd been there before. This was different because it felt as if God was working non-stop, and while obedience brings blessing, it can also bring weariness as a natural by-product if you're not careful.

One morning, I had been preaching at another meeting somewhere, and a few of us decided to swing by the tent on what we thought was a short "recharge and refresh" break, just to see what was going on, grab the other men and go get something to eat.

The second my food hit that property, I felt a twist in my gut. I needed to go pray. As simplistic as it sounds, I went down there just to pray and before I knew it, I found myself immersed in what was quite possibly the deepest moments of prayer I had ever experienced in my entire life to that point. For 20 minutes, I lay there in prayer with this complete calm. It wasn't loud; it wasn't boisterous. It's hard to give it a name because it was such a surreal feeling.

Brother Daniel said he thought that moment was God giving me the power to preach to the thousands. I don't know if that's what it actually was, but here's what I do know: God fills you with the Spirit, and that day God gave me fresh oil. That day, God gave me fresh strength just like He gave Elijah that day under the tree as he rested. After that moment I was revived and ready to keep on pushing for this revival; to keep fighting the spiritual war that comes along with every great thing that God wants to do through us on this earth.

A NEW MINISTRY TAKES SHAPE

Youth Night was supposed to be the end of the revival—at least, it was on the timeline we had established when we set up the tent. But, once again we found ourselves at the crossroads, trying to decide if we should continue on or not. We knew that God wasn't done there, but we made up our mind that it wasn't going to be just me and Brother Randy deciding whether to continue. So, as soon as that youth meeting ended, we met with those pastors right away. We needed them to be behind it with their people. After all, they were moving their Wednesday night events and services, and all their people, so we were nervous about how it would be received.

All those pastors sat up in the choir loft in the chairs facing us at the pulpit. Finally, all these men came to us and said, "We've got all that you need." Once again, all the pastors were in complete agreement, without exception.

But that created another challenge. We had already extended the meeting twice, and we wanted to be able to plan accordingly this time. But we knew that we had to give the tent back to Brother

Ralph at the beginning of August, so that he could prepare for his own meeting that followed. So we began looking at options to continue the meeting after the tent was gone. Everywhere we tried, the doors wouldn't open. The Greensboro Coliseum would have been affordable at that time of year, but it was under construction. We priced out renting a tent and all the equipment, but by the time it was all said and done, it would have cost us seventy thousand dollars just to rent it all for a few weeks.

We were out of options that we could fathom, so one night, we were in a meeting with all the pastors, worrying out loud about what we would do about continuing the revival. Then, the unimaginable happened—one of those older preachers spoke up: "Well, instead of renting it all, I'd rather just buy CT one."

Before I share with you my feelings on that, it's important to rewind a bit. A few weeks prior, in one of those morning prayer meetings, I walked in and Daniel had asked me to stand in front of all of those pastors. I was a little nervous because I had no idea what he was going to do, to be honest. Then he uttered these words: "God's put this in my heart: God's gonna launch Brother CT into the crusade ministry." I heard him, and all the while I'm wondering, "What in the world?" I haven't prayed for a tent; I didn't even like preaching under a tent at that point in time! It's hot out there; let's go to a church with air conditioning. But every time I'd get around them, that's what they'd say: God's gonna give you a tent.

So now, with yet another man of God confirming this, I was a bit rattled. For the first time, it clicked. "I don't really want a tent." You know what I mean? That's not what I want; it's not what I had in mind for the future of our ministry. We were a small ministry; I had one staff member, and now we're talking trucks and trailers and all that—how was I going to pay for it all, let alone deal with all that?

The reality was, back when the meeting was still at New Hope and someone mentioned putting up a tent, I was the one to say, "Absolutely not." It was June. It was 90 degrees outside. For me, I never wanted to be in the tent ministry. I thought it was outdated; people don't want that. Needless to say it's something they used to do…people don't have a desire for that anymore. But when we put that tent up, people from all over the place came, and it somehow served as this unexpected bridge, connecting our past and our heritage and an older generation to our future, and with new generations. No man could have planned that or thought that up, let alone believed it would work. God, in His infinite wisdom, didn't share it with us along the way. Instead, He unfolded it through obedience and there we were, once again standing in awe as we connected the dots, realizing what God's plan was all along.

While it wasn't our first choice all along to make tent ministry a big part of what we thought we were building, we yielded to what God wanted to build for us, in us and through us. By yielding to that, we learned more about God's wisdom and His "why" behind the idea. We began discovering that we could go into a town and reach scores of people who would never step foot into a church building. For some, this was because of prior hurts and experiences in church. For others, who had never had experience in church, it was for fear of the shame or condemnation they feared they'd be subject to behind the front doors. And for others, some just never felt worthy enough or cleaned up enough to be accepted in church. Right or wrong, the feelings exist and they're real strongholds on people. Rolling up to a tent, though, is pretty unassuming. It gives people the safety of feeling as though they can slip in the back, or the side, observe and slip out unnoticed and unjudged if and when they so choose.

As I struggled with all of it, I reminded myself of the promises God had given me. I remembered the moment when God told me one morning in prayer that He was going to shift my ministry to not just focus on young people, but to give me an audience to influence another generation. Even with that in my mind and heart, and surrendering my will to His, I said, "Lord, if you want me to have a tent, then you'll have to give it to me." I also was thinking that there was no way we'd ever raise that much money, so I really didn't have to worry about it, because if you don't have the money, you can't buy one. It's supposed to be as simple as that.

…But God.

So out of obedience, I tasked a bunch of guys to look into it. I said, "Take a couple of days and see how much it's going to cost, so at least we have confirmed our fear. Then we'll tell the people on Friday night so they'll understand that it isn't a realistic option." When they came back with a number of two hundred and fifty thousand dollars, I just laughed and said, "Okay, let's tell them then."

When God said that we have not because we ask not, by the way, apparently He wasn't playing around. That night in church, Brother Daniel and Brother Randy got up and said, "We can't deny what God's doing, and none of us think that this is the last time that CT's gonna need a tent like this." So they gave the people the numbers and told them to be prepared for the next week to give as God led their hearts to participate, with no pressure. Then they sat back to let God do what God does.

We got on Facebook live, and told our audience there what we were doing. We then came up with the idea to offer people to sponsor poles for different amounts, and offered plaques for poles bought in memory of someone—all this stuff to try and raise this money. And, in miraculous form, people started sending money from everywhere. Before we ever received the offering that next Friday night, to my astonishment, we had raised one hundred thousand dollars—all of which had come from people that believed in what we were doing, and sent a love gift in to help us.

Still, I couldn't imagine us being able to raise another hundred and fifty thousand dollars. But before I knew it, during the offering, Mr. Hursey got up and said, "I'll give fifteen thousand dollars, if y'all can match it."

And that started it all, like a pebble that starts an avalanche. People started bringing their offerings to the Lord instead of us taking up one; they just walked up to that altar and started laying money down…laying promise cards down. There weren't one or two massive donors; it was just everyday people giving a little bit; whatever they felt led to contribute.

Over the course of that week, the money kept pouring in. During the service, we received a strange call, one that came all the way from New Zealand. I remember thinking…New Zealand? Where is New Zealand? They were on a seventeen-hour time difference, but still watched the live stream every day. When we talked to them on the phone, they were weeping—these strangers from across the world—and they were fighting back tears saying, "We've never seen anything like this, but we've watched every single service and we are believing God will do something like that here. We want to give some money." And then they asked, "Would it be okay if we sent you ten thousand dollars?"

That next Friday night, while I was still in the pulpit, men were in the back totaling the pledge cards and offerings to arrive at a final count. Finally, they handed me a piece of paper with the number of the actual giving on it.

I was dumbfounded.

Over three hundred and twenty five thousand dollars was raised that night. When it was all said and done, every dime we needed was provided to purchase a brand new tent, chairs, equipment, and the tractor trailers to haul them in! All this for the sole purpose of providing our ministry with a tent—the one thing I never wanted, but the very thing God knew that I would need. Burlington Revival had become so much more than just a revival for a small city. In that moment for me, it launched our ministry to places and people I never imagined.

PULLED OVER
AND LIFTED UP

During our time under the tent, we regularly hired police to help secure the meeting. Local law enforcement was so very helpful. One night while I was preaching, God burdened me for those police officers. They were standing in the back, doing their jobs, seemingly unengaged from anything I had to say, but focused on what they had to do. So I began preaching to them. I don't recall my exact words, but I said something to the effect of how thankful we were for them, and how while they may think that they are only there to work, God might have other plans. I shared that God can save people in uniform working the same way He can anyone else.

They never moved. None of them ever testified of accepting Christ, but on one of the last nights of the meeting, I was pulling out onto the frontage road headed back to our bus, and a police car pulled out in front of me abruptly. At first I thought I had done something wrong. The officer walked up to my window. He introduced himself and told me about how he had "worked the tent" many nights, and how he appreciated all we had done in that town. He asked me if I had time for him to share a story.

"One night under the tent, as you straight up started preaching to the cops that were there…sir, that night you were talking to me. Mr. Townsend, I was afraid I would get in trouble if I went down to the altar, but that night standing in the back I bowed my head, and did what you said, and I asked Jesus to forgive me and to save me!" He then began to tell me how God had radically changed his life, and how he went home and made things right with his wife, and how the entire direction of his home was changed.

Tears streamed down my cheeks as I got out of my truck and hugged that officer and prayed with him. What an incredible testimony. I thought to myself, how many people are out there just like him, that we have no record of, but just the same trusted Christ during that meeting. Only eternity will reveal all that God did during those days, but I will be forever grateful for the night I got stopped by a policeman and heard how he got saved.

THE
REVIVAL ENDS

When people ask us how the Burlington revival ended, we typically respond in only one way: Like a funeral. Although every single one of us felt at peace when it was all over—we knew we had done what we had been called to do—we had been to memorial services that were far easier than that moment in time.

In the end, we didn't close it down because we couldn't get along. We had simply exhausted our efforts trying to find a new location; all doors had shut to us on every avenue, and so we knew it was time. The burden I had previously felt—that I might be sinning if we stopped—disappeared. I lost that, and felt a calm as it ceased to be my responsibility; it was out of my authority, and we were at peace about it.

At the time, some wondered: are they missing God? And of course, being human and also loving God and wanting to lead people to Christ, we struggled with the same question...would we feel later like we were missing God? But what we found out was that when we look back on it all, the way it all played out, everybody obeyed

God. If we had missed God and kept going and the whole thing flopped because we didn't have a tent, or for any other reason, there would have been doubt and confusion about so many things that had happened already. What we thought at the time was failure was really the future, because we wouldn't have raised that money without it. In the end, if there hadn't of been a need, there wouldn't have been the provision that launched a ministry to bring revival like that with tent ministry to communities all over as a result. What we thought was the end was really the seed for a harvest we are only beginning to experience, all because of the grace of God, His glory, and the obedience of so many to seek His will. The final night of the meeting, I communicated this message. Burlington is not the end, it is the beginning. If anything, what God did in Burlington gave us hope that God still can move in our day.

Following the revival, we formed a committee and tasked them with handling all the money. We would've done that anyway, but especially since the news had been involved and had reported how much money was raised, we knew it was not only critical to handle every dollar honorably the way we'd always do, but it was even more important to ensure complete transparency every step of the way, so nobody could make any outrageous false claims like, "Oh, that CT, I bet he went and bought a jet" or "a new car" or whatever else comes on the back end of such an incredible financial miracle. It was not just important to ensure my reputation and those of others in leadership connected with Burlington weren't tarnished; we could live with the typical finger pointing. It was most important to all of us to ensure God got all the glory, and His reputation remained untarnished and beyond reproach. In fact, even though we had done our due diligence on the front end, when we actually had to start buying things like the tractor-trailer and cameras, we discovered that we had significantly under-budgeted in our haste to try to corral ballpark estimates quickly. So when God gave us that four hundred and fifty thousand dollars, He knew we needed every cent.

God proved once again to us, through the Burlington Revival, that He still can do a supernatural work in these dark days. For so long, all the church has talked about is what God *has* done, but not about what God *can still* do. That summer, it was as if God flexed his muscles and said, "Look, if you do things My way, submit your will to Mine, stay fervently united in prayer, remain humble and obedient and step out courageously on faith, I can still move in a supernatural way. I can break out of the walls of religion, and do these things and more."

In the end, everything that happened at Burlington was not something that we could take credit for, or say that we planned and expected. Burlington was a series of supernatural breakthroughs, the likes of which we may never see again the rest of our lives in that kind of way. Then again, He promised to do exceedingly, abundantly above all we can ask, think, or hope for, so maybe... just maybe...He'll do it again. Maybe, in fact, He'll do it for you, in your church, in your community, despite your inadequacies, your ill-preparedness, your under-resourced vision and your limited expectations that He can do something you've never seen in your lifetime.

THE RIPPLE EFFECT OF REVIVAL

In the days and nights of the Burlington Revival, we have record of one thousand, two hundred and fifty people that came to the altar, meaning that we took a Bible and showed them how to be saved, and they declared to us that they trusted Christ and were saved. And if that were all that those twelve weeks produced, it would have been more than enough. But in reality, the ripple effect was far wider than that. After all, people came from sixteen states (at least, that we recorded), and watched from countries and cities around the globe online.

Tyler Gaulden, Pastor at Church Street Baptist Church in Greensboro, North Carolina, later shared this story in a letter to me:

> *The best way to describe my day-to-day ministry was that, prior to the Burlington Revival, we were going through the motions. I had been pastoring for three years, and had experienced typical growth at our church, but down deep inside, I knew here was something that was missing. I couldn't put it into words, and certainly had no idea how*

to put it into action, but I knew I wanted more, and I knew it was something supernatural. I couldn't explain what that meant because, quite frankly, I'd never seen it happen. I had read about it, but I had never seen it with my own eyes until the summer of 2016.

I went to New Hope on the first Tuesday night of the meeting, and things seemed normal. There was an average size crowd and the service was what I'd expected. When you (CT) stood up to preach, you did a great job as usual, but it still felt like this was going to be a typical meeting, God would show up, and lives would be changed. That is, until Friday night. Something happened had never seen before. I certainly couldn't put it into words but in my spirit, I knew exactly what I was seeing; something supernatural. Over the course of the next sixteen weeks, my life, my family, and my ministry were forever changed. The moving of the Holy Spirit that I witnessed night in and night out confirmed in my heart the true power of the Holy Spirit. I watched as sinners wept for salvation. I watched as preachers wept for unction. I watched as churches wept for revival.

The Burlington Revival became the benchmark in my heart to know the true power of the Holy Spirit. No longer do I go through the motions, because I feel no need to; I feel no need to make it happen and I feel no burden to run the show. My hope has turned to being filled with the same Holy Spirit that I watched work for sixteen weeks under that white top on the side of that highway. My church, my ministry and my heart have been forever changed. Some people will describe the summer of 2016 as the summer of

*the Burlington Revival; but I will always describe it as the
summer when I saw the supernatural.*

Pastor Jason Dowdell, a Pastor in Sanford, North Carolina (an
hour away from the tent site), saw over a hundred people from
his community saved—people he had bussed into the meeting.
During that same time, his congregation grew from under two
hundred to well over three hundred. His youth group—the seed
of a next generation's revival—went from fourteen to forty-five
during those same few short weeks. But what is most telling is
the result of those salvations among those teens. When the youth
leaders began planning a game night, the kids begged to organize
a Bible Study night instead.

As a parent myself, it infused me with a renewed hope for my kids,
knowing they got to experience that. One time during the meeting,
my son Tucker ran down to the altar where I was standing. He had
a Bible in his arms almost as big as himself. He's usually sitting in
the back by his momma, but that night, he came running down
the aisle and he said, "I'm gonna lead me somebody to Jesus
tonight, daddy." Now, he can't even read that Bible, but he's been
seeing all these souls being won, and he was intent on being down
there waiting for them. To this day, we'll be in church and Tucker
will see somebody acting weird and he'll say "Dad, they're under
conviction." So as a father, it gives me hope that my kids have seen
God move in an unmanufactured church environment.

If you look back throughout the Bible, you'll find story after story
of great moments in history where God interceded on man's behalf,
and where great miracles happened in the midst of the seemingly
impossible of situations. Abraham and Sarah had a baby when

they were a hundred years old. Moses and the Red Sea, Jonah and the fish, Daniel in the lion's den, and on and on and on. We look at all these individual events in people's lives in scriptures, but we forget that many of those accounts were only, in many cases, a handful of days—a sliver—in each of their lives. One single event, and everything God did before that led up to that one day played as important a part in the future that was to come. So when we look at the Burlington Revival in the grand scheme of history, just as we're instructed to rightly divide the scriptures, remember to look at the events and testimonies of Burlington in perspective; it is just a sliver of a greater story that's still being woven together by God, much of which perhaps we may never know as a result of the ripple effect of so many people's faith, prayer and obedience.

The point I realized how far reaching the ripple effects of the Burlington Revival might extend hit home well beyond the point it had ended. The second year we were there, Becky came down with a rare illness, and no doctors could figure out what was wrong. We went from doctor to doctor, specialist to specialist, all baffled. She spent seven days in the hospital; we were desperately trying to figure it out, but there weren't any answers, despite some very caring, talented of physicians.

Finally, we brought Becky before the church to pray for her. One of the things we prayed was for God to give us favor with the right people who could send her to a big enough hospital that specialized in diagnosing things that others couldn't figure out. We didn't know much about medicine, but we did know God. Shortly thereafter, one of the men who prayed for her mentioned having a couple of nurses in his church from Duke, and said he'd see if he could make something happen there."

Before we knew it, I received a call from a complete stranger, a lady named Miss Nell, who turned out to be the personal assistant to the chief surgeon at Duke. She was very professional, took notes on what was going on, and ensured me she'd call back soon. I didn't really think we'd hear back from her, but within a few hours, she called back. "We have an appointment for you, here at Duke, on…"—it was all set up. A door was kicked wide open that we'd prayed for but had no idea could actually happen. I was so choked up with gratitude, I could barely talk.

"Ma'am, I'm grateful, but why in the world are you going through such lengths to help us from such a long distance?" The phone went quiet. Finally, she said, "Brother CT, you were preaching underneath that tent the night I got saved."

God's provision for Becky's healing had been lined up long before we even knew we'd have a problem.

The doctors at Duke quickly figured out what was going on and Becky was moved to the top of the list for surgery—a surgery that the surgeon told us was a nine on a scale of difficulty of ten. In fact, they cautioned us that we could count on less than one hand the doctors in America who could have performed the surgery, so there were certainly risks.

At that hospital, though, it was surreal. I could not take fifteen steps down a hall without somebody stopping me. I'm talking about patients, orderlies, employees, nurses…all coming up to me with tears in their eyes, all telling us how Burlington had changed their lives. I counted thirty-five people that day alone that came up to me and shared with us that they had been saved at the Burlington

Revival. I can't explain the emotion that came over us that day, but I sure was thankful that I made that call to Chattanooga to ask Brother Broom to allow me to stay in Burlington. I'll never get over what God did in my heart during the Burlington Revival.

Today, a few years later, we're still regularly experiencing that ripple effect. In the past as we did meetings, the room would always have been about three-fourths full. Now, when we go back to those same churches, you can't find a seat. And it's not necessarily me, but everybody knows what happened in Burlington, and they come with expectation that God will do what He said He'd do, over and over again.

BURLINGTON IS ONLY THE BEGINNING

As we left the property one final time, and the tent came down, there was a unanimous resolve in our collective hearts. Burlington was not the end, it was just the beginning. God did not do all this and give us all this equipment, and favor, and relationships, and so much more, for just a few months of impact. We believed, and still believe, that God has big plans. Since Burlington, a fresh hope has been birthed in so many churches; a newfound belief that God can still send revival to His church. Some said that in some ways, for them, Burlington was like taking a step back in time, and I'm completely fine with that. Without a doubt, there are things that the church of today has abandoned from the church of yesterday that we should have held onto. Effectual fervent prayer, the power of God on the music and preaching, and an opportunity for souls to be saved are non-negotiable for me.

I've been asked so many times, "How do you go back to having normal church after something like the Burlington Revival?" I don't think you can, and for that I am thankful. Many young people will never be fooled by a shallow, emergent church philosophy now.

Once you've been in the fire, the smoke will never satisfy. God not only gave us a hope; He gave us a hunger to see God do it again.

> *"Wilt thou not revive us again:*
> *that thy people may rejoice in thee?"*
> — Psalm 85:6, KJV

Many theologians have debated, with eschatology in mind: Can one last revival actually take place? Can America see revival again? Adrian Rogers said, "Study the history of revival. God has always sent revival in the darkest days. Oh, for a mighty, sweeping revival today." Can revival happen? I have had many a man look me in the face and tell me it isn't possible. However, I believe Dr. Sexton was dead on with his comments early in the forward of this book and that we have seen, and will continue to see, God use revivals to mark both our history and future. We will continue to bring our families, our communities, and our nation back to our roots for His glory, with great anticipation of what He'll do, what He'll restore, and who He'll deliver.

I also believe what E.M. Bounds said: "God has, of His own motion, placed Himself under the law of prayer, and has obligated Himself to answer the prayers of men."

God can do whatever He wants to do. God is God, and He is pretty good at being God, so let's leave Him in that seat. On our end, it's our job to do the praying and staying obedient. It should be the desire and prayer of every born again Christian to see real, heaven-sent revival fall in this land one more time! Our world is in turmoil, our nation is in trouble, and our churches have lost the tender touch of revival. It doesn't matter who we put in

Washington D.C.. Neither a Democrat nor a Republican has ever been—nor will ever be—capable of fixing or healing the deep-rooted wounds that sin has placed upon our soil. America has turned its back on God time and time again, and we have too often forgotten the God of our fathers. We've witnessed the forsaking of the house of God by so many generations, and forgotten the prayers of the saints that got us to where we are today. America isn't a great nation because of our money, military or manpower. America is what she is because of the divine supernatural hand of God that has blessed us.

Is revival possible? I pray so. But let me tell you what I know is possible. It is absolutely possible for you, the reader of this book, to experience personal revival. Pastor Lee Roberson once said, "Revival begins in the individual's heart. Let it begin with you, on your face, alone before God. Turn from every sin that might hinder. Renew yourself to a new devotion to the Savior."

It is possible for you to draw nigh to God, and He will draw nigh unto you! Cleanse your hands, get everything out of your life that grieves the Holy Spirit, and let God set your soul on fire. Revival. I know without a shadow of a doubt that it is possible. One thing about a soul on fire for God—it spreads. That's when we pray for that wind in Ezekiel 37; "Come O' Breath!" Let God breathe on that fire, and the fires of revival spread. That's what we need. Lord have mercy, our children need to see a real move of God, our churches need to see a real move of God, as do our marriages, and our families. We are in desperate need of revival.

Personal revival, fervent prayer and a God that hears prayers is very possible. In fact, that, simply put, is what happened in

Burlington, God set the hearts of people on fire, and the fires continued to spread. I love to think of the possibilities of many of those coals still simmering, awaiting to catch ablaze as the next breath of God blows through them.

Leonard Ravenhill said, "As long as we are content to live without revival, we will."

Our hope and our prayer is for this book is that this book will build your faith to believe that God still can do the miraculous, and that the stories of what God did in Burlington would stir you to seek God's face for revival in your city. We also pray that the testimonies of lives changed would provoke you to get back in your prayer closet, and pray another prayer, and that the burden that was so heavy on the people in Burlington would transcend through the pages of this book, and become your burden. Do it again, Lord, do it again!

> *"For I will pour water upon him that is thirsty, and floods*
> *upon the dry ground: I will pour my spirit upon thy seed,*
> *and my blessing upon thine offspring:"*
> — Isaiah 44:3

I leave you with the challenge to rekindle your fire, renew your hunger and thirst for Him, and recommit your pursuit of His righteousness.

> *"Blessed are they which do hunger and thirst after*
> *righteousness: for they shall be filled."*
> — Matthew 5:6 KJV

ABOUT
CT & BECKY
TOWNSEND

Raised in the mountains of Charleston, West Virginia, CT grew up in the home of a pastor. After graduating high school from Fair Haven Christian School, he attended Pensacola Christian College for one year. After returning home, CT enrolled West Virginia State University and began chasing a business degree.

At the age of 21, God changed all of CT's plans and called him to be a gospel preacher. Just a few months later, following God's will, he moved to North Augusta, South Carolina, and enrolled in Victory Baptist College, worked on staff as an assistant to the pastor, and earned his bachelors degree in Pastoral Theology. It was while he was attending Victory that he fell in love and married Becky. With the blessing of pastor Dr. R. Larry Brown, Victory was the launching pad of their evangelistic ministry.

In 2012, CT had the privilege to work under the leadership of Dr. Ralph Sexton, Jr., at Trinity Baptist Church in Asheville, North Carolina, as an assistant pastor. It was here that God began to implant deeper the burden for evangelism and revival.

CT and Becky and their three children, Tucker, Syler and Everlee, now live in Anderson, South Carolina, and are members of Temple Baptist Church, where Becky's father, Dr. Steve Hurte, is the pastor.

CT TOWNSEND
MINISTRIES

Today, in addition to their weekly revival itinerary, CT Townsend Evangelistic Ministries hosts a number of Gospel preaching events that carry God's message of love, grace, and forgiveness to men, women, and children across America and internationally.

Whether they are filling auditoriums and reaching young people through the Carolina Youth Rallies, preaching to thousands during the summer, at the Arise Youth Conference and Carolina Youth Camp, or working together with churches in area wide crusades, CT Townsend Evangelistic Ministries is passionate about clearly preaching the Gospel to as many people as possible.

For more information, visit CT Townsend Evangelistic Ministries on the web at www.cttownsend.com.